2014
THE BEST WOMEN'S
STAGE MONOLOGUES

2014
THE BEST WOMEN'S
STAGE MONOLOGUES

Edited by
Lawrence Harbison

SMITH AND KRAUS PUBLISHERS   2014

ISBN: 1-57525-888-9
ISBN: 978-1-57525-888-1
ISSN: 2329-2709

Typesetting and layout by Elizabeth Monteleone
Cover Design: Borderlands Press

A Smith and Kraus book
177 Lyme Road, Hanover, NH 03755
Editorial 603.643.6431 To Order 1.877.668.8680
www.smithandkraus.com

Printed in the United States of America

FOREWORD 11
Lawrence Harbison

A COMMON MARTYR 13
Michael Weems

A KID LIKE JAKE 15
Daniel Pearle

ABOUT A WOMAN NAMED SARAH (2) 16
Lucas Hnath

ADULT 18
Christina Masciotti

AND AWAY WE GO 21
Terrence McNally

BABY BIRD (FROM *MOTHERHOOD OUT LOUD*) 23
Theresa Rebeck

BIKE AMERICA 25
Mike Lew

BITE ME 27
Nina Mansfield

BODEGA BAY (2) 28
Elisabeth Karlin

BROADWAY OR BUST 32
Rosary O'Neill

BROKEN FENCES (2) 34
Steven Simoncic

CORE VALUES 38
Steven Levenson

DEAD AND BURIED 40
James Mclindon

DIFFERENT ANIMALS (3) 41
Abby Rosebrock

DONKEY 46
John Patrick Bray

ERECTILE DISFUNCTION 48
David L. Epstein

EXQUISITE POTENTIAL 49
  Stephen Kaplan

GEEK (2) 50
  Crystal Skillman

GOOD TELEVISION 53
  Rod McLachlan

H20 54
  Jane Martin

HARBOR (2) 55
  Chad Beguelin

HEART SONG (2) 57
  Stephen Sachs

HOW TO MAKE FRIENDS AND THEN KILL THEM 61
  Halley Feiffer

HOW WATER BEHAVES (3) 62
  Sherry Kramer

I WANNA DESTROY YOU 68
  Joshua Conkel

JERICHO (2) 69
  Jack Canfora

LAST FIRST KISS 73
  Chad Beckim

LEVITICUS 75
  Bekah Brunstetter

LOVE ON SAN PEDRO 77
  James McManus

LOVE SICK (2) 79
  Kristina Poe

LUCE 81
  JC Lee

MATA HARI (2) 83
  Don Nigro

MR. BURNS 87
  Anne Washburn

MUD BLUE SKY 89
  Marisa Wegrzyn

NEW IN THE MOTHERHOOD
      (FROM *MOTHERHOOD OUT LOUD*)   92
  Lisa Loomer

NO WAY AROUND BUT THROUGH   94
  Scott Caan

NOOHA'S LIST (FROM *MOTHERHOOD OUT LOUD*)   95
  Lameece Issaq

ON THE SPECTRUM   97
  Ken Lazebnik

OUT OF THE WATER   98
  Brooke Berman

POLLYWOG (2)   99
  John P. McEneny

QUASARS   102
  Jennifer O'Grady

SAMARITANS; OR WHERE IS SYLVIA?   103
  Wayne Paul Mattingly

SEVEN INTERVIEWS (2)   104
  Mark Dunn

SILA   108
  Chantal Bilodeau

SKIN AND BONE   110
  Jacqueline Goldfinger

A SNOWFALL IN BERLIN (2)   112
  Don Nigro

SOMEBODY/NOBODY   116
  Jane Martin

SOUSEPAW (2)   118
  Jonathan A. Goldberg

SOUTH BEACH BABYLON   121
  Michael McKeever

STELLA AND LOU (2)   122
  Bruce Graham

STUPID FUCKING BIRD   126
  Aaron Posner

SUNSET BABY   128
  Dominique Morisseau

TEA WITH EDIE AND FITZ   130
  Adam Pasen

THALASSA   131
  Scott Sickles

THE BEAUTIFUL DARK   132
  Erik Gernand

THE BOXER   133
  Merridith Allen

THE CURIOUS CASE OF THE WATSON INTELLIGENCE (2)   135
  Madeleine George

THE FARM (2)   139
  Walt McGough

THE HIGH WATER MARK (2)   143
  Ben Clawson

THE HOMOSEXUALS   147
  Philip Dawkins

THE JACKSONIAN   149
  Beth Henley

THE LAST SEDER   151
  Jennifer Maisel

THE SINS OF REBETHANY CHASTAIN   153
  Daniel Guyton

THE SNOW GEESE   155
  Sharr White

THE TOTALITARIANS (2)   156
  Peter Sinn Nachtieb

THE TRIBUTE ARTIST   159
  Charles Busch

T.I.C. (TRENCHCOAT IN COMMON)   161
  Peter Sinn Nachtieb

TOURISTS OF THE MINDFIELD   162
  Glenn Alterman

TROPICAL HEAT   164
  Rich Orloff

UNDISCOVERED PLACES (2)   165
  D. Richard Tucker

VEILS (2)   169
  Tom Coash

VERY STILL & HARD TO SEE   171
  Steve Yockey

WARRIOR CLASS   173
  Kenneth Lin

WILD   175
  Crystal Skillman

YEAR OF YHE ROOSTER   177
  Eric Dufault

YOU ARE DEAD. YOU ARE HERE   178
  Christine Evans

ZOMBIE RADIO   180
  Don Nigro

RIGHTS AND PERMISSIONS   183

Here you will find a rich and varied selection of monologues for women from plays which were produced and/or published in the 2013-2014 theatrical season. Most are for younger performers (teens through 30s) but there are also some excellent pieces for older women as well. Some are comic (laughs), some are dramatic (generally, no laughs). Some are rather short, some are rather long. All represent the best in contemporary playwriting.

Several of the monologues are by playwrights whose work may be familiar to you, such as Don Nigro, Theresa Rebeck, Terrence McNally, Jane Martin, Sharr White, Bruce Graham, Beth Henley and Charles Busch; others are by exciting up-and-comers such as Merridith Allen, Lucas Hnath, Jennifer O'Grady, Crystal Skillman, Jacquelyn Goldfinger, Jonathan A. Goldberg, Dominique Morisseau and Eric Dufault.

Many of the plays from which these monologues have been culled have been published and, hence, are readily available either from the publisher/licensor or from a theatrical book store such as the Drama Book Shop in New York. A few plays may not be published for a while, in which case contact the author or his agent to request a copy of the entire text of the play which contains the monologue which suits your fancy. Information on publishers/rights holders may be found in the Rights & Permissions section in the back of this anthology.

Break a leg in that audition! Knock 'em dead in class!

Lawrence Harbison
Brooklyn, NY

Dramatic
Maddie: Twenty to twenty-five

Maddie returns from a shopping trip and springs her new lingerie and confessions upon Randall, who has secretly hooked up with Maddie but continues flirting with her sister, Lee.

MADDIE: This is my seventy-five dollar bra. You like it? Correction. This is my seventy-five dollar "love me, fuck me, or at least goddamn notice me" bra. Did it get your attention? Because it seems like nothing else will. I thought you were different and you thought I was one of the guys. But you knew better. I was gracious to a fault. Forgiving. "Maddie doesn't mind if we talk about butts and racks and who goes down faster than a knock-kneed goalie." What would Lee have been for you, Randall? A conquest? Would she be the one who drove sixty miles in a thunderstorm to see your game? Or the one, who no matter how many times you struck out or sat on the bench, still thought you were a good player? Would she be the girl who spent hours with you at the batting cage on a Friday night, pumping tokens into that damn machine and *still* saying, "Good job." Are you going to miss me when you're gone? Probably not. In a few years and trying to start a career and you're bored with some trophy wife —I won. I think that's the moment when you realize that you actually love me. Who am I kidding? It's water off a duck's back. I'm a consolation prize. Do you deny it? Did I make you crawl into my tent? And did you think I would be your little secret—someone you can only treat like a girl when the lights are out and no-body's watching? You honestly thought the next day you could go back to "good old Maddie" and mess my hair like some little kid? I bought this get up today, thinking there might be something else for you and I. Never in my life have I spent so much on a goddamn bra. You know how I justified it? You deserved it. I may not be much to look at, but this silly thing sure makes me look filled out. Doesn't it? I used some of my graduation money. Now math isn't my strong suit. But, now that I know we won't hook up again, the ratio in my mind becomes clearer. Seventy-five dollar bra versus five inches of *(she giggles)* temporary bliss.

Dramatic
Judy: fifties

Judy is a preschool director who advises parents on how to get their kid into a top elementary school. She is talking to Alex, the mother of a precocious 4 year-old boy who loves Disney princesses and dress-up games.

JUDY: I had a new parent, the class below Jake's, the *father* came in about an hour ago, no appointment, no phone call, nothing. Wanted to know why his son isn't learning more "pre-reading" skills. More math . . . I swear to God. He waltzes in with his power suit, Rolex, sits down like he owns the place and tells me, "They're just playing all day! I'm paying thirty grand for a playroom." And it's like: Hello?! Your son is three years old. Playing is how he *learns,* you pig-head. I said, "Well sir, *you* may not value imagination or creativity but actually both are foundational for all types of higher learning. You see a kid pick up a block and use it like a cell phone? That's abstract thinking right there. That's the basis for abstract language." Well believe it or not, his son's actually adorable, go figure. And normally it wouldn't have gotten under my skin but this whole week's been like that. We've got prospective parent night on Monday. It's just insanely tight this year. I did a panel last week over at Hunter, there were three of us talking about the moral imagination of children under five. It wasn't even about education per se, but of course, immediately after I had a swarm of these parents asking—how many openings, how many slots. And, you know, I could deflect or be vague but instead I tell them the truth and suddenly, boom, I'm the enemy. "That's *it?* That's *all* you have?"

Seriocomic
Sarah: Forty-four

Sarah Palin is being considered by Sen. John McCain to be his running mate in the 2008 presidential election. Here, she tells him why she would be a good choice.

SARAH: Because I have problems, and because we ran out of money, and because Todd didn't have a job, and people run out of money, and people don't have jobs, and that's normal, and we're normal, and—can I say something? You're not normal. You're not normal. You're special. You're up here. And I'm over here. And I'm special. I'm also special, but different, in a different way, I'm—and God made me special, but I'm also normal. I look normal. I seem normal. I act normal. You don't act *not* normal, no, I mean, but you're something else. It's good to be something else, that's how God made you, but it's also good to be normal. I'm not saying you have to be normal, I'm saying, all I'm saying, is: I'm useful, because I'm so normal that I'm special too, and I'm tough, and I'm strong, and I fire people, when people work for me, and they don't work out, when they have bad character, when they don't work out, I fire them. I cut them off. I make decisions. So yeah, I've got that working for me too.

Information on this playwright may be found at www.smithandkraus.com. Click on the AUTHORS tab.

Seriocomic
Sarah: Forty-four

Sarah Palin is being considered by Sen. John McCain to be his running mate in the 2008 presidential election. Here, she tells McCain's wife Cindy why she would be an excellent choice.

SARAH: Making decisions, managing people, hiring people, firing people, deciding what needs to happen, deciding what's best, and deciding how to decide what's best, and picking people to help me decide what's best, and deciding how to decide who to believe and who not to believe, because everybody wants you to believe them, but not everybody's right or not everybody's idea is right at the right time. And then there's deciding how people need to be told about your idea of what's best, to make them see what's best is best, and to make them see that the other ideas aren't what's best, and deciding what people need to know and what people don't need to know because not everybody needs to know everything all the time, and that's not lying, that's just—because telling them some things would only confuse them. And then there's deciding when what needs to happen needs to happen, and who should do it, and who should watch them do it, and how they should do it while they're being watched doing it. And then when you're done, figuring what you've done, and what worked and what didn't, and how to let people know what worked, and how to not let people know what didn't work, because not everybody needs to know everything all of the time. That's it, isn't it? That's all it is.

Information on this playwright may be found at www.smithandkraus.com. Click on the AUTHORS tab.

Dramatic
Tara: Eighteen

Tara, a college freshman, hates where she goes to school because she thinks it full of cardboard, cookie-cutter phonies. She has come to her father, who has a gun shop in his home in Reading, PA, basically to hang out and talk about her life. For him, Reading is a rapidly deteriorating nowheresville; for her, it just what she needs for a while.

TARA: I feel like my life is going around and around in a very small circle, and never advancing at all. I just feel like everything is so lame. I'm living a person I don't wanna be. I'm eighteen. I don't wanna be eighty and be like, I just did what I was supposed to. I mean college isn't what people think it is. The key to opportunity or whatever. There's so much bullshit going on. Yeah, it's great if you wanna be brainwashed into all this commercialism and money hungry country, stay in school. I just don't see what's the point. I don't see my life going anywhere with it. What could I do in ten years? Mediocre job. High rent. Loan payments on top of everything. I wanna experience my life. I don't know. I've always been afraid of change. Right now, I want my life to turn completely upside down. Like even just being back here, I feel like a different person. I feel more of who I really am. *(pause)* Actually, I was thinking about taking a semester off, and maybe staying here a while. I don't know how to explain it, but I mean the second I got off the bus, I felt so connected to myself. It's beautiful. You can see the sky. There're trees. It's like so natural, like I don't need to use materialistic things to make me happy. I can see why people spend their whole lives here. I don't know what I wanna do for my life, and I don't know where I wanna be ten years from now, but right now, I wanna be here. I wanna be in the middle of nowhere. So, what do you think?

Information on this playwright may be found at www.smithandkraus.com. Click on the AUTHORS tab.

Dramatic
Tara: Eighteen

Tara has left her freshman year at college to decide what she wants to do with her life. She has been living with her father. Turns out, she has a boyfriend whom she wants to go and visit but she needs bus fare to get there. Her father, not happy with her choice of boyfriend, doesn't want to give it to her.

TARA: You never reached out to me. You sent birthday gifts through snail mail so they came a week late. You think that counts for anything? It's more personal communication like using Skype or FaceTime that makes a difference. How dare you stop paying child support when I turned eighteen. You washed your hands about me. All you do is pay my phone bill! You buy me a phone for my birthday, something from the dinosaur time, you didn't even pay twenty dollars for it. I looked it up on Ebay and the bidding started at ninety-nine cents! After a year of dry spell you look for extra work. It doesn't work that way, the bills keep coming in. You have to find work. You're not the only one with financial problems! You took money under the table not to pay child support! We had to petition the court. Checks came. Eleven dollars. Twenty-four dollars. I don't know why Mom endorsed them, fold and tear, fold and tear, fifteen dollars! Wow! Thanks, Dad! Mom was starting a business on her own. One person worked for her who she couldn't pay. We had to move to pay for my first semester of college. We had to move to a smaller place. You didn't pay for my education. One thing I need your help with, and you can't do it! I didn't know how lucky I was to be spared any fucking connection to you.

Information on this playwright may be found at
www.smithandkraus.com. Click on the AUTHORS tab.

Seriocomic
Anne Tedesco-Boyle: Forties to Sixties

Anne is a new board member of a theatre company on the rocks, here meeting the company for the first time.

ANNE TEDESCO-BOYLE: That's all right, gentlemen, don't mind me, I'm a new board member, Anne Tedesco-Boyle but everyone calls me Annie. Theatre is my addiction, I'll be quiet as a mouse. Zip!
    (She zippers her mouth but can't resist one final encouragement.)
"Lay on, Macduff!"
    (to us)
I love these open rehearsals when it's not about the results and it's about the process. They've drummed *that* into our dear little heads.
    (to the actors)
Really, don't mind me, I'm invisible.
    (to us)
I joined the board of this theatre to be a part of the creative process, even if that means primarily giving them money. I'm not a creative person myself and I certainly don't pretend to understand the creative process but I've been drawn to both ever since I saw my first play: *Peter Pan*. When Tinker Bell was dying and Peter asked us to save her, no one clapped louder than me. When Shirley Channing invited me to join the board, I was hoping to change my relationship with these fascinating people. So far, it hasn't. They're grateful for my support—"Thank you, Mrs. Tedesco-Boyle"—but I've never had a satisfactory answer when I asked an artist what it's like to create. It must be wonderful. Well, there's a whole new season ahead to answer that question, our forty-ninth consecutive one, I guess I can say "our" now, including

my favorite play, *King Lear* with my favorite company actor, John Pick. I should know what play you're rehearsing. *The Country Wife*, of course, our first play of the season.

(to us)

Is there anything more fun than a Restoration Comedy? Or, as Candace Delbo, our dramaturg says, is there anything more restorative? That Candace! I don't have to remind you: these are difficult times. More than ever we need art in our lives to get us through. It's all yours, gentlemen.

Information on this playwright may be found at www.smithandkraus.com. Click on the AUTHORS tab.

BABY BIRD (FROM *MOTHERHOOD OUT LOUD*)

Theresa Rebeck

Seriocomic
Woman: Twenties to forties

A mom has two children, a boy and a girl. Her little girl, Cleo, is Chinese and is adopted, which confuses all the other moms in the park when she refers to her children as brother and sister. Mom is fretting about how to explain all this to Cleo.

WOMAN: You know I was, actually, there was one day when Cleo told me she was worried about all the other babies in China. She was four at the time and she was worried that their parents would not find them, the way we had found her. So I told her that the Chinese government was very good, very efficient, and that they knew how to get the right babies to the right parents. Which made her feel better, but I did realize that she thought that that was where all babies came from—orphanages in China. I worried about this for weeks. My husband finally said: What are you so worried about? And I said, I am going to have to tell her that some babies come out of their mother's stomachs. And that in fact her brother came out of *my* stomach, and she did not, she came out of *another* woman's stomach, in China. Don't you think that will upset her? And my husband said: Well, no babies come out of my stomach, so I never actually thought about it.

(*Beat*)

I did tell her. That sometimes babies came out of their mommy's stomachs. She thought this was hilarious; she laughed and laughed. So I said, yes that is funny but you know, your brother came out of my stomach. Which gave her pause. And then she said, "I wish *I* came out of your stomach." So we talked about it for a little, and she went off to play. Then that night, when I was putting her to bed, she said to me: You know what I wish? I wish Cooper came from China. And I said, yes, that would be the other way to level the playing field. But whether or not you came out of my stomach, you are my baby bird, and I am your mother.

Dramatic
Penny: Twenty-seven

This monologue comprises the final scene of Bike America. *Penny, our plucky protagonist, has just spent the last three months on a cross-country bike trip from Boston to Santa Barbara. She's never lived anywhere but at school or her parents' place, and she's been hoping the trip would help her to find herself, and to find a place that feels more like home. Instead, she finds her life and her trip cut short when she is run over by a truck while biking alone in the night in the middle of the Arizona desert. In a direct address to the audience, Penny now wrestles with what, if anything, she's learned from the journey.*

PENNY: What's up you fuckers I'm dead. Do I have any regrets? Yes. Would I do it again? No. The truck driver phoned in the accident just after he *awoke from the wheel.* That was thoughtful. He realized he'd turned his fifty-three foot trailer into a forty-four thousand pound penny-crushing machine. You remember those penny-crushing machines they have at museums where you put in fifty-one cents and out comes a flattened penny shaped like a scenic vista? That's pretty much the deal with me. After the usual freakouts, the group pressed on and found the Pacific. They dipped their raw, weary feet in the waves and mumbled platitudes like, "Penny really would've liked this." And I'm like—yes. Yes, I would've liked this. I would've liked this a great deal more than being *smeared out like toothpaste* on the Arizona highway. And I felt these waves of regret at being a fuckup. And I felt these waves of regret at all the time I spent looking outwards, all that deflection when I should have just loved and lived. And I could have loved. Anyone. And I could have lived. Anywhere. Anywhere down that four thousand mile expanse. There were four thousand Pennies all down that route and yet I had to go and pick that one. They stood there, their feet in the sand, feeling the waves that I'd never feel, watching a sunset I'd never see. And they smiled and nodded like they knew me. And I thought, how could they know me? I still don't know me.

Information on this playwright may be found at www.smithandkraus.com. Click on the AUTHORS tab.

BITE ME
Nina Mansfield

COMIC
Ellen: Mid-twenties to mid-thirties

Ellen has managed to subdue a vampire with pepper spray (who knew you could do that?) and brought him home in a cage. Her husband has told her he wants them to spend all eternity together. Here's his chance.

ELLEN: So there he is, stunned from the spray. Writhing on the ground like a baby. When WHAM! Got him in the balls. BAM, I hit him with my handbag, and ZANG, got him again with the pepper spray. At that point it was like pure adrenaline! I was on fire! Once I had him subdued I realized the emblem on my Tory Burch handbag is totally cross like, so I held it up to his face, and sure enough he was like, *Ahh*, and I was like, "take that you creature of the dark," and he was like, *Ahhh*, and I was like, "that's what you get for attacking women in alleys," and he's like, *please, I can't help it! It's just my nature*, and I'm like, "I don't care if it's just your nature you woman hater," and he's like, *please, I don't hate women, I just want to suck your blood*, and I'm like "ew," and he's like, *you get used to it*, and I'm like "really?" and he's like, *really*, and then he started to lunge for me again, 'cause I'd sort of forgotten to hold up my handbag, but I was like really caffeinated, so my reflexes were on point, so I was like, "take this!" and he was like, *Ahhh*. And then I had this idea. I thought, why not take lemons and turn them into lemonade. I was like, "you scumbag vampire," and he was like, *I'm really not a scumbag*, and I was like, "Oh yeah?" and he was like, *yeah*, and so I sprayed him with more pepper spray, and made him drape my handbag over his shoulder, which made him lose like all his powers, and then I loaded him into the back of the Escalade and Voila!

Seriocomic
Caroline: Twenties

*Caroline is a receptionist. Her mother calls her and she
tells her a story about another woman who works at her
office.*

CAROLINE: Mr. Kern's office, this is Caroline . . . Ma, I
have like no time to talk now. I'm here by myself and . . .
No, Teddy didn't call me today . . . But listen, you know
the other girl who works here? . . . You know, the quiet
one, with the glasses . . . So like, she calls this morning
and she's like "I have to take some time off" out of the
blue, you know? So I'm like "whatever" and . . . Ma,
you know who I'm talking about, we're the only two in
the office aside from Mr. Kern . . . What does she look
like? I don't know—she looks like . . .
    (Takes a beat to recall.)
. . . I don't know, she looks average, no it's more like...
you know, plain. You know, with those big glasses. But
the thing is she literally hasn't taken a day off since I've
been here and she picks now to suddenly go somewhere?
. . . You don't see the problem? Well because she knows
I'm getting married . . . No, she's not married, what does
that have to do with anything? . . . I don't know, cause
who would marry her? She's dull. She literally has no life
. . . What do you care where she went? . . . Look, I can't
talk, I am so stressed right now . . . What stress? Hello?!
I'm here all by myself and Mr. Kern, he doesn't care, he
expects me to . . . Will you stop about Teddy already? You
know, he doesn't have to call me every minute of every .
. . I'm not getting hysterical! . . . I don't want a valium!
Will you just listen a second, I'm here by myself and . . .
How would I know? It's not like we're friends . . . . Ask
her to lunch? Are you serious? . . . I don't want to get to

know her . . . Ma, can we stick to the subject . . . Hello? My wedding? . . . No, it's got nothing to do with Teddy. Teddy's fine. We have a good relationship, I mean he's marrying me right? Nobody's putting a gun to his head, right? . . . I mean, right? . . . You know what? *You* take a valium . . . Nothing is the matter, who said anything was the matter? . . . No, it's just that I've got a lot to . . . No ma, you want to know what my problem is?

(on the verge of tears)

I'm getting married and nobody seems to care!

DRAMATIC
CARLOTTA: FIFTIES

Carlotta is a fortune teller. She is talking to a woman named Louise who has come to her for help in finding her mother, who has disappeared.

CARLOTTA: I see a car . . . a small beige car. This woman gets into the car with a man who drives. It is a wooded area with very tall trees and yet I can hear the ocean. They drive through the trees. The car stops. They get out of the car and walk. They are walking on a trail that goes through the woods. It's like what you call a short-cut. And this man . . . this man . . .
  (She shudders.)
I feel so much anger around him. He despises women. He is a woman hater. I think he has a plan. He walks fast and she must run a little bit to keep up with him. Oh, he tells her they are going to a bar for a drink. Aha! That is the lure . . . that is the plan. They walk and the trees are clearing and I can see him now. He is young, of typical height, hair that is brown. I see a blue jean jacket.
  (Beat)
Wait! Now I see . . . in the woods . . . I'm seeing washers, dryers, old refrigerators. It is a place where people throw junk. Far off there are some old trailers but nobody lives there. They are alone, she and the man in the blue jean jacket. There is no bar. There will be no drinks. And now she knows. She feels it in her stomach. She knows she is in danger.
  (Beat)
She is afraid and knows she must run—It is too late. Her body is in the water, floating in the sea and she has become a part of it. Her body and her pain . . . so much pain . . . is a part of the sea. The sea surrounds the pain. I see

the blue jean jacket running away through the woods.
(Beat)
And everything goes black.
(Beat)
You go home now. Go back to your island. There is danger all around you here.

Dramatic
Susan: Seventeen to twenty-six

Susan, a breast cancer survivor, is trying out for a part on Broadway. Here, she talks to the auditioner.

SUSAN: I want to live to seventy or eighty or fifty. I don't see why I have to talk about my illness to get cast in your show...I don't want to go back there because it's a long road it's not just remove THIS, it's a panoply of choices and any one could kill you. No one tells you how complicated it is 'cause you'd be scared out of your mind. I just want to act. Get to Broadway. I don't have time for mindless chatter. Take me to dinner and I'll jabber away. I need back up because with "Team Love" we can really pop open this room. I'm one of six children, the *unpreferred* one. Just 'cause I'm pretty and a girl doesn't mean I can't be direct. I don't want people dumping my pictures and resumes into garbage after I . . . because acting is my opiate against death. If I go to Broadway, I won't die. Look at me. It's the theatre community I'm after. There are people dying. There are people being born. But I have died before I died. So Broadway has to let me in. This is the last irrelevant thing I'm going to say. I'm an actor with a life threatening disease and still I got to . . . face these extended, labyrinthian auditions. Maybe this call back will cause a relapse. Or steal my beauty years. Do you know what's it like to fear a slow death. I'm an artist, someone trained to think in images, to become deeply sensitive. I'm scared to lift my arm and find some strange pain or new lump or weird bruise. I can't go back to life where it's struggle, struggle, struggle. Sorry we don't need you, you're not right, maybe next time. I got to trick my mind, replace the bad thoughts, make myself dream a future. Give me the part.

Dramatic
April: Mid-thirties

*April has convinced her husband Czar to move into a gen-
trifying neighborhood in the heart of Chicago's deep West
Side. The neighborhood has proven to be dangerous. This
monologue is her self-audit of how she got here and why
she made this choice. It is delivered to the audience.*

APRIL: I am invisible. Been invisible all my life. When I
was a kid I could go days, weeks, without being seen.
Dirty brown dishwater hair and flat-ironed features
wrapped in bad posture and functional shoes. A "B
student" with a "B cup" from a sanitized suburb whose
most extraordinary feat was a perfect attendance plaque
and a Charlie hustle award at basketball camp. An upper
middle-class, middle-of-the-bell curve, too-quiet-to-be-
tragic, too-boring-to-be-bulimic, forgettable flavor with
an academic-alcoholic dad and a trophy-wife mom. So I
tried to make myself be seen. From slut, to goth, to punk,
to priss, to princess, to yogi. I hijacked identities and wore
personalities like catholic school girl skirts. Until they
had to see me—incomplete and stereotypical—silly and
pathetic—like a dream catcher on a dashboard or a tattoo
of the word "hubris" on the small of your back. Search
and destroy, damn the torpedoes, cut your forearm with a
kitchen knife and blow away a coffee-stained guid-
ance counselor . . . be seen, be obscene, be witnessed, be
intervened . . . until one day an ordinary man makes an
extraordinary effort to make you feel smart and pretty.
Enjoy being seen through his eyes. Stop sleeping with
his friends and start sleeping with him. Get bored, get
routine, get for granted, get honest about the fact that
you never stopped being invisible . . . until a little stick
turns blue and forty-six chromosomes turn you inside

out for the whole world to see . . . Transform. Transcend. With your thick hair and your swollen ankles—your bloody gums and your linea nigra—until who you are, is no longer what you were. A tangible, fragile, dirty brown dishwater B-student, B-cup . . . mommy . . . something singular and specific, authentic and committed . . . drunk with responsibility and dripping with identity. Find a house that looks nothing like the one you grew up in. Force the issue. Fake the answer. Convince *an ordinary man who makes an extraordinary effort* that you are right . . . even if you aren't sure. Because . . . for once . . . you *need* a place to be seen.

Information on this playwright may be found at www.smithandkraus.com. Click on the AUTHORS tab.

Dramatic
D: Late twenties, African American

*D Coleman and her fiancée, Hoody, have lived in Garfield
Park their whole lives. As the neighborhood gentrifies, their
property taxes have increased and they can no longer afford
to live in their own home. This is D's recounting of her life
and struggle for survival that continues to this very day. It
is delivered to the audience.*

D: I am invisible. Been invisible all my life . . . spent
years moving through the shadows and cracks of broken
men and angry boys too proud to ask for help . . . and
too arrogant to say thank you when you give it to them
anyway. Fierce, black and strong, I watched the pride lion
puff up and go out into the wasteland only to come home
and explode. Sixty-four. Fantastic, tragic fireworks filled
with bravado and machismo, his wives and daughters,
circling his fire, soothing his burns, stroking his face,
and whispering sweet relief between the pounding in
his ears. Hoody enters her light and pulls the hood back
off her face. A beat later he takes the sweatshirt off her
shoulders, puts an industrial cleaning smock on her,
and leaves her light. And when the noise stops, and the
darkness fills the room, I show up, like I always do . . .
in the shadows and the silence, with a bucket and a mop.
Bandage a baby brother's bloody hand . . . Steady daddy
as he pisses Hennessey into a jelly jar 'cause he's too
drunk to stand. I clean up the glass. Lock the door. And
turn off the light. Then I wrap my feet in Vaseline and
impossibly puffy white socks, and I disappear under my
sheets. My ashy skin now soft and serene. Because I do
not need to be seen. *(Beat)* I need to be heard. From baby
cry to lullaby life isn't what you see. It is what you hear.
And when you a two-month cocoa brown baby girl left

alone in a second story walk up—you need to be heard. So I cried until they heard me. And when your cousin takes you under the freeway, and no one can hear you over the roar of the trucks on The Kennedy, you need to be heard. So I screamed until they found me... until I found my own voice. Simple and clear. Louder than you'd expect. And it was *fierce* . . . almost beautiful. But now . . . I have gone silent once again. Six community meetings and three trips to the Cook County Assessor and I still cannot be heard. Two loan officers and a local news reporter . . . *and I still cannot be heard.* A half hour alone with a tax bill and an alderman . . . and I still cannot be heard. So every night I come home tired and hoarse—having lost my voice again—to say good night to a proud man who always listens but doesn't always hear. And when the house goes quiet, and the night is silent, I whisper . . . to momma. Tiny prayers and promises of survival that sound only like me. Because I know she can hear me . . . and I know she loves the sound of my voice.

Information on this playwright may be found at www.smithandkraus.com. Click on the AUTHORS tab.

Dramatic
Eliot: Early twenties

Eliot has had a tough time finding a job out of college, but she's just been hired by a corporate travel agency which, it turns out, is on the ropes. She is on a team-building retreat with her boss and two other employees, one of whom has just asked her about her employment history.

ELIOT: I've been applying to probably two jobs a day for the last four months probably.
  (As ELIOT speaks, she begins at some point to cry.)
But they wanted experience, all the jobs, and I don't have any experience, I guess. I mean, I went to college, and I always thought that was experience, but it's not apparently. Everywhere I go, they're like, well can you do Excel? Can you do PowerPoint? And it just
gets to the point where you're like, I can't even get a job at Bed Bath & Beyond. Like literally, I tried to get a job at the Bed Bath & Beyond near Union Square and I had an interview and I thought it went pretty well, but then they never even called me back, because I didn't have enough experience. Even though I had a lot of experience in selling, in making sales, I worked at the art gallery for over three and a half months, until it *closed*, which was not my fault that the owner was a cocaine addict, but they said selling art was different, it was a different kind of skill set from home goods and they were worried I would have a hard time adjusting, in terms of skill sets. And I was, like, that's not true. And they were, like, well, we think it is true. And I was like, there are skills I have that could be really valuable to you. And they were like, like what skills? And I was like, like my personality. I have a really good personality and I'm personable and I can talk to people from all walks of life and I went to a

really good college and I'm smart and if you teach me how to sell home goods, I can sell home goods, I swear to God. And they were, like, we disagree. And I was like well you're totally wrong. And they were like well actually *you're* totally wrong and we're the ones who get to decide, so yeah, don't call us, we'll call you.

Information on this playwright may be found at www.smithandkraus.com. Click on the AUTHORS tab.

DEAD AND BURIED
James McLindon

Dramatic
Bid: Forties to fifties

Bid is the supervisor of the grave-digging crew at a cemetery, consisting of two teenagers. Turns out, she got into the field when she served in the Marines. Bid's goal is to dig graves at Arlington National Cemetery. Here, she tells her two charges about her military experience.

BID: Marines. M.A.U. Mortuary Affairs Unit. Body retrieval. Body prep. Well-placed munition'll spread four bodies over a thousand square yards in three seconds. We'd do the retrieval, put 'em in body pouches. Just like a crime scene: Lay out your grid, walk your grid, put a little flag on each body part—Four jigsaw puzzles mixed together. Sort the parts out. Make each one whole. (*Pause*) Whole as you could. Sometimes whole would've fit in a baggie. Technique was all that kept you sane, kept you from thinking 'bout what you were really doing. Arlington's a way to finish all that. (*Pause*) It comforts a mother, to see her child laid dead and buried down in a row with his brothers and sisters. In formation, guarding each other, holding each other. Doing what she can't do anymore. The ceremony comforts her, wraps its arms tight 'round her, holds her together. It's so beautiful. Taps. Volley of shots. Flag folded taut. White stone taking its place in the rank, in the file. All that holds a mother tight, the way she once held her child. (*Pause*) Tells a mother she can't wail, can't tear her clothes, gives her the strength not to. She can hold formation cuz the formation holds her, keeps her sane. Keeps her safe. She needs to be kept safe from herself. Needs to have the pain made orderly, the death made orderly, to manage it. That's what we do, that's what Arlington does.

Information on this playwright may be found at
www.smithandkraus.com. Click on the AUTHORS tab.

Comic
Molly: Late twenties

Molly Gardner has agreed to accompany her coworker's unfaithful wife, Jessica Tarver, to a South Carolina abortion clinic. Here, Molly recounts how her obsession with Jessica's husband led her to obtain evidence of Jessica's affair with the Tarvers' pastor.

MOLLY: I asked Leo a while back what kinda car you drive. Just so I'd know. Then a few weeks ago when I was jogging down Ezell Boulevard I saw a red Civic in the parking lot, and I thought, Maybe that's Jessica Tarver's Civic. I should run in there and get some cheesecake and bump into Leo and Jessica. And if they look super in-love I can just go ahead and kill myself . . . But anyways I knew what you looked like from Leo's pictures, and you were nowhere to be found in the dining area, so I just decided to pee and get outta there. But lo and behold, I'm in the bathroom stall, peeing, and I hear this man's voice going like, *Jess, Jess*, and I'm like, *Jess!?* Could it be? And it was! So I just snuck into the next stall and watched the whole thing through a crack. Man, when he pressed you against the door and hung you up by your shirt on the little coat-hanger, I was like, I have to try that!

Information on this playwright may be found at www.smithandkraus.com. Click on the AUTHORS tab.

Seriocomic
Jessica: Late twenties

Pregnant, friendless and freshly rejected by her pastor-turned-lover, Jessica has enlisted her husband's coworker and love interest, Molly, for moral support on a trip to the abortion clinic. Here, as the women are getting to know each other, Jessica explains why she has always been superstitious and in the process reveals her deep-seated dread of being alone.

JESSICA: The day it came out Meg Ryan and Dennis Quaid were splitting up, I saw something about it on a hospital TV, and it was just weirdly devastating to me, and I thought, This has to be a horrible omen. Otherwise I wouldn't feel so bad about it. And then my mom died later that afternoon, and ever since then I've been like a crazy person . . . You know what's always scared me? I'm not saying my dad flew off into somebody else's arms right away; he didn't. But right after she died . . . Sorry for telling you this; I'm in a weird mood . . . But after she died, all these middle-aged women started just . . . coming out of the woodwork, throwing themselves at him. I'd see it at church and my aunts' and uncles' parties. And I got to know a handful of them when he started dating, and they were all just so desperate. None of them were attractive, they had this . . . shellacked hair, and I remember thinking, Honey, you know not to use that much hairspray! I know you know that; have you not seen a magazine in twenty years!? What's happened to you!? And they weren't far from our age now, Molly. One of them was thirty-three! And that's when I figured out . . . If it'd been the other way around, if God forbid my dad had died, and my mom had been the one to survive, there wouldn't be any men lining up to marry her. She'd have been alone for the rest of her life, just getting fat and doing ridiculous shit to her hair.

Information on this playwright may be found at www.smithandkraus.com. Click on the AUTHORS tab.

Seriocomic
Molly: Late twenties

As Molly and Jessica await Jessica's appointment time at the abortion clinic, Molly confesses the extent of her devotion to Jessica's husband.

MOLLY: Well, let's see. After I got fired from teaching, when I got the job at the library, I thought it'd just be awful. But then they're taking me around the office floor introducing me to people, and I see your husband sitting next to an empty cubicle. He was punching things into an old-fashioned calculator. And honestly my first thought is: If the seat next to this man is for me, I know I'll end up falling in love with him, and I'll have to go through tons of just that crushing, unimaginable pain, but a lot of wonderful things and pure ecstasy will come out of it too, if I'm patient. And lo and behold, the seat's for me, and within weeks he's confessing things all the time; he's telling me how much he hates being broke and having dropped out of college, he feels like a failure, he misses driving out to the beach and surfing, he thinks he's too grumpy towards you. And in my head I'm thinking, Marry me, Leo! Leave your wife and let me drive you all the way out to the beach and watch you surf and let you be grumpy and show you how sexy and perfect your brain is. And one afternoon I was crying at work because I was thinking about my mom—that only happens like once a year—but Leo touched my arm to make me feel better, and he slid his hand up just a microscopic fraction of an inch underneath my sleeve. It was this short-sleeved red cardigan from Ann Taylor. I could tell he was enjoying it because we locked eyes and a tremor went through him. It was a sexual tremor; it made his fingers press into my skin. And when he felt my whole body react he laughed this quiet little laugh for a second or two because he was so proud, he knew I'd never been so turned on by anything in my life, and if it weren't for his wife he could pleasure me so much more, for however long I needed. Ever since then I've kept myself awake at night with this vision of Leo's mouth opening up to laugh. Just thinking of it—I need him to pin me down with his body and hover over me and protect me and fuck me! God . . . damn, it was his kindness that brought all this on, Jessica! His kindness to *me*! I've been with some other men, okay? I have, but Leo makes me feel the opposite of how they made me feel. I just wanna thank him, I want him so badly, Jessica, I wanna give myself to your husband so badly. I love you for being his wife, if you had children I'd love them for being his children, I love every single object you've bought together and used together! I think of all the precious little things inside your home that you depend on together, and yes I'm jealous of them, but I love them!

Information on this playwright may be found at www.smithandkraus.com. Click on the AUTHORS tab.

DONKEY
  John Patrick Bray

  Dramatic
  Eloise: Twenties

Eloise, a struggling slam poet, addresses Steve, an indepen-
dent coffee shop owner in upstate, New York. After learning
that the third-party mayor has paved the way for a corporate
coffee shop to move into the center of town, Steve alien-
ates the community, rather than proving his store's worth
(and his own). Eloise has just entered looking for one of
his regulars, PenTdragon. Steve attempts to blow her off,
which prompts her to say the following:

ELOISE: How come you're such a miserable asshole, man?
  You were doing MJ. Yeah, we all know it. Walked in on
  you once. Should lock the doors. Respect, you know? I
  even thought about joining.
      (She starts delivering, almost like a slam.)
  It looked like. A saturated phenomenon. You know
  what that is? It's a religious experience. It looked holy.
  Sublime. More than me. Different than me. Something I
  guess I long to be. She had this look on her face, like she
  was torn out of a French film. She could've been in black
  and white, the way she looked dreamily out the window.
  Then, she blushed, and I had to smile. And when it was
  done, man, I wish you would light a cigarette. A fiery lay
  deserves some smoke. You feigned indifference. I don't
  know why. Turned on the lights, let the customers in,
  and I don't think I ordered anything then. I just wanted
  to be in the room where it happened. But I look at you
  now. You're a shell. You're a nothing. And you know it.
  Where did you go? Hustling coffee, pretending that none
  of us are affecting you, because the truth is, maybe we
  do. Maybe we do just too much. That's why you pushed
  us all away. We could save you. Save your shop. Create
  an event that would let everyone in town know you're

here for us. But the problem is, you really aren't because you won't let yourself be. You've been holding that towel a long time, waiting for the first flimsy excuse to come along, to let you toss it in, so you could play the victim. You're a poser, Steve. You're not a businessman. You're not a coffee man. You're a man who wants to be a victim. And I don't want any part of that.

Information on this playwright may be found
at www.smithandkraus.com. Click on the AUTHORS tab.

Comic
Mira: Thirties

Mira is a professor at a prestigious university having marital troubles. She thinks her husband is involved with one or more female students. In this monologue, she vents to her best friend.

MIRA: Do you know why they call it that? They call it Viagra because it rhymes with Niagara. The advertiser is saying to aging alpha-males everywhere, "you're gonna be so good that she's gonna cum like Niagara Falls"—A place famous for honeymoons and synonymous with sex. And why do they use a "V"? Why not a "B" for Biagra or a "C-H" for Chi-agra. No. They use a "V" for Viagra because V stands for Vagina! Or what about Cialis? The other drug. Why do you think they named it that? They're saying that when you pop this pill, you're going to cum so hard you're going to "see Alice" . . . As in, *Alice in Wonderland*, a cute little blonde in a blue dress? And who are they distributing this wonder blend to? Baby Boomers with hair falling out and Woodstock tickets fading in a shoebox next to their signed Hendrix poster. The heartbreak hits when the next commercial comes on and we're walking through some third world alleyway and some man who looks like Santa Claus is trying to get me to feed the children for twenty-three cents a day and I think to myself—Viagra was invented before we put a stop to world hunger?

Information on this playwright may be found at www.smithandkraus.com. Click on the AUTHORS tab.

Seriocomic
Laura: Early thirties

Laura's husband Alan thinks their three year old son David is the Messiah.

LAURA: Even if he is the Messiah we can't tell him. We can't tell anybody. We have to keep it a secret. Alan—if you love me. If you love David. If you love our unborn child—we will not talk about this again. It's not a question of if I believe you or not. But I will not talk about it again. It's too big for me. I will support you and I will help you and I will help our son and I will help our daughter and I will open myself up to the possibility of this, but I cannot talk about it again. Ever. Please. That's not saying whether it's true or not true, it's just saying that this is the end of it. Out loud. Never. OK? We love him. We don't treat him any differently. We do what we did when we brought him here today—go through our routine—and if he's the Messiah then there's nothing we can do that will stop that. Look, I don't know much about the New Testament, but Mary and Joseph didn't really have that much to do with Jesus' path to Messiah□hood, did they? I mean there's no talk about anything different they did with him than they would have with any other child. They taught him to be a good person—to be caring, to be loving, to treat people with respect, to stand up for himself, to think freely—aren't we already doing the same things for David? The only way we're going to screw him up is if you tell him that you think he's the Messiah. Nobody can live up to that. Even if they are the Messiah. We teach him that he is but dust and ashes and also that for his sake the world was created.

Comic
Minnie: Young teens

Minnie, a young teenager cos-playing (dressing up!) as a minotaur monster, jumps into this cos-playing "fight club" (run by fifth graders!) to battle Danya and win a chance to meet her biggest idol at Dante's Fire Con: the creator, Joto Samagashi.

MINNIE: I'll crush you! I know all of minotaur's moves. I've been working on 'em. I love the ladies. I love the cheeseburgers. I still wear my Dante's Fire glow in the dark underroos—you know the one with Ulee—o and Dante flying through the stars and Cleo following them with her red ax of fire and I'm ready to go in!! To win! To go straight down. See Samagashi! I'm ready! I'm ready! YES! Took the bus. The bus broke down. Found a car. Smashed through. Don't know how to drive. Got out of the car. Ran. Little old lady found me—thought I looked cute and petted me and called me Maxie poo and I let her. I let her. Door opened. Ran out. Guards. So mean. Wanted money. So much money. Ran to ATM. Ate my card. Kicked it. Screamed. Calmed. Thought: What would Samagashi do? Sold my entire Dante's Fire first series right there in front of those Geek Gestapo. Said they needed exact change. Ran to deli. Got banana. Potassium! Ran back. Threw the money. Ran. And now victory! I'm ready to win now Brian!!!

Information on this playwright may be found at
www.smithandkraus.com. Click on the AUTHORS tab.

Comic
Honey: Thirteen

*Honey has been racing through Dante's Fire Con (an anime/
comic book convention dedicated to her favorite story) to
meet the creator—her idol Joto Samagashi. She is cos-
playing (dressing up!) as Virgie the co-star of the show. She
has just gotten into a huge fight with her best friend (who
is cos-playing as Dante), and fought two awful older lady
cos-players who stole her bag with something very special
inside. Here she speaks to her new friend who helped her
get the bag back—some kid playing Squeaker, a cute orange
fuzzy "pack-man" like creature who stays in character all
the time—and we learn the darker reason of why she and
Dante came to the convention today.*

HONEY: We got my bag back—yes! Oh man whoever you
are—you are the best! When I am Virgie I am the best! I
am!! A trusty right-hand gal and guide who always knows
everything and where she's going and is so confident and
cool!! Right? Right!
    (Clutches bag)
Well, thanks again. I bet you have to go. This place closes
in like twenty minutes—I can't imagine you want to
spend your last few minutes with a stranger. Most people
think your character, Squeaker, was put in the *Dante's
Fire* TV show to use as exposition so my character Virgie
could spill her guts when everything went wrong. And
man, why is everything going so wrong? We got what
we wanted and I could totally make it to Samgashi now
on my own—I know I can now but—oh! I don't know
what to do. I know this isn't your problem but—You
aren't going to take your costume off are you. You're
going to keep playing—Because you obviously spent a
lot of time on that costume! You've even got some spy-

looking, super faraway hearing device in there—because that's Squeaker's skill! O.K. Squeaker? I've been pretty mad lately. And now I've got what we made—
(She opens the bag and shows what's inside: a lovingly decorated DVD case.)
We put together all the videos—what my sister and Danya and I—we've been working on for so long. It's all our own—all the moments with all the Samagashi characters we love. It's what we wanted to show Samagahshi—that was the plan until . . . It's really messed up, and I don't have anyone to talk to . . . ! I just need someone to listen. My sister and I we came home from the park after the worst day we'd ever had. I was crying . . . she . . . She didn't cry. She took off her Cleo armor. Her jacket. She sat there in her jeans and t-shirt in front of the mirror. "Leave me alone Honey." I was pissed she wouldn't talk to me. I slammed the door. That was the last time I saw . . . A week ago my sister died. She chose to. And we choose to come here like it's some kind of quest, like if we meet Samagashi—like that would change anything? But whatever choice I make now—I make on my own. And I'm not anything like Virgie, but it is—it's making me who I want to be! And who cares if I get laughed at for liking the coolest kid in school? Like that's going to work out—being in love with Bobby Branden. I know there's no way the cutest guy in school would ever be into me but—Well, I know you love me Squeaker, I raised you from an egg on the planet of Glock!

Information on this playwright may be found at www.smithandkraus.com. Click on the AUTHORS tab.

Dramatic
Brittany: Twenty-eight

Brittany is trying to impress a woman named Connie, who produces a TV "reality show" about addiction, with her family's sad story in hopes of getting on the show. Clemmy is her brother Clemson, who is a crystal meth addict.

BRITTANY: Clemmy was a oops kid. I'm seven years older and Twotus is, like twelve years older. He barely saw Clemmy grow up. I tried to protect Clemmy, but about when I was seventeen, just about ready to start my last year of high school, my Dad's landscaping business went to shit. And he was drunk all the time, got real out of control . . . so that was fun. Clemmy was always . . . so aware, ya know? He could always feel what was going on before I could. We were close back then, and we'd walk home from school together, and he could tell there was trouble by just opening the door. Daddy never let up on him. You know, it just ruined Clemmy. And I miss him, I miss that sweet little brother I used to have. But that's all gone, now. He's high all the time, he's steals everything not nailed down. Goes through my purse, sold all of Momma's jewelry. Even her wedding band. I got two kids with no daddy, no help. I'd like to finish nursing school, but I got to keep my job. Mom's getting worse, now she's smokin' with her oxygen on. Twotus ain't any help. We're beyond broke, and I'm so tired I could just die. Look, Clemmy's got to get better or I don't know if this family's gonna . . . I can't take care of anybody else more.

Information on this playwright may be found at
www.smithandkraus.com. Click on the AUTHORS tab

H20

Jane Martin

Dramatic
Deborah: Twenties

When she arrived to audition for Jake's production of Hamlet, *he had just slit his wrists. She called 911 and saved him. She has just learned that the production is to proceed, and she has been cast as Ophelia, even though she never auditioned. Jake, a movie star, is a cynical who-gives-a-shit kind of man, for whom life is a meaningless, endless farce. Not for her.*

DEBORAH: I'm not in a farce, Jake. Sorry. I am in my life in God's service. I've been in New York for four years and I have done eleven Shakespeare's in parks, and parking lots and prisons and an abandoned hospital and I have never gotten more than bus fare, so my story is a little different than yours. Until two months ago I lived with seventeen women in the dormitory of a Christian hostel. I have seventy dollars in checking and nine dollars in my bag. You think you're a joke? I won't do plays that don't enable God's handiwork, now let's see you make a career out of that? Oh, and I don't take handouts. You want an argument for the existence of God, try Shakespeare. He transcends man while showing what man could be. Which by the way, Mr. Abadjian, you don't. So despite the fact I would commit . . . sins . . . to play opposite Dawnwalker, because everybody who is anybody will come to gawk at you, and I will blow them away and have an actual career that I can use to fill my heart and bring people to Christ. But I'm not going to demean my talent and purpose so you can feel better about your infinite confusion and wasteful life.

Information on this playwright may be found at
www.smithandkraus.com. Click on the AUTHORS tab.

Dramatic
Donna: Mid-thirties

Donna, a sometime singer and full time screw-up, has shown up in Sag Harbor along with her teenaged daughter Lottie at the house of her brother Kevin and his husband, Ted. Donna is homeless and she and Lottie live in a van. Kevin is an aspiring novelist who is totally supported by Ted. He has asked Donna to read his manuscript. Here, she comments on it. And, by the way, she's pregnant again and wants Kevin and Ted to take her baby.

DONNA: You wanna know why you're so blocked on your book? It's because you're afraid that if it isn't published, you're going to be forgotten. That's the problem. There's going to be no one around to remember you. Your story just ends. But when you have kids, you're immortal, Kevin. You're part of something eternal. Without that, what have you got? It's just you and Ted growing old in this scary museum of a house and then just dying someday with nobody caring. It's the saddest story ever told. I've known you much longer than Ted and you've always wanted to be a father. Well, technically, you always wanted to be a mother, but from the looks of things around here, we're not far off. The point is, I'm worried about you, Kevin. You're going down a path that you never wanted to go down. Here's your chance to have your cake and eat it, too. Ted will understand. I've seen the way he looks at you. He loves you. And who knows? Maybe it'll give you something to write about. Wouldn't that be nice? And obviously it'll help me out. I mean, I can't raise another baby, look at how I fucked Lottie up six ways from Sunday. I'm in a bit of a panic here, too, you know. I can't be in a band with a baby. I can't sing on a cruise ship. So I'm just going to have to give it away anyway. You want your unborn niece to go to strangers?

Dramatic
Donna: Mid to late thirties

Donna, a sometime singer who lives in her van with her teenaged daughter Lottie has shown up in Sag Harbor at the house of her brother Kevin and his husband Ted. She is pregnant again and she wants them to take her baby. Kevin is amenable to the idea, but Ted is adamantly against it. Kevin has decided to leave with her and Lottie in the van, but Donna is trying one last time to persuade Ted not to let that happen.

DONNA: Yeah, yeah, shut up, I know. I'm trying to rectify this cluster fuck of a situation, okay? You think this is what I wanted? Now I'm gonna have three kids to take care of. Whether you like it or not, there's a big gaping hole in Kevin's life. Just say yes to him. I'll stay here for a few months. Not here, but someplace close by and cheap. I'm sure Sag Harbor has a Howard Johnson's or something. And then after the baby comes, Lottie and me, we'll be on our way to the Caribbean or Alaska. I'll sing "Besame Mucho" to fat Americans, Lottie will get to see the world and eat buffet style shrimp. Our life will be all shuffleboard and ice sculptures. And as for you? You'll hire a nanny, it won't be so hard. And those scrapbooks of yours! They'll finally come to life, man! You'll have a little girl to eat your stained-glass gingerbread houses! Instead of going to the movies on Christmas, you'll be waiting for Santa! Think of the birthday parties and the cakes and the letters from camp and the dance recitals! Just say yes, Ted! Why are you fighting it?

Dramatic
Daloris: Fifties, African American

Daloris is a five-year cancer survivor living in Harlem, New York City, taking a flamenco class for middle-aged women in the East Village. After class, she tries to convince newcomer Rochelle about the healing power of flamenco.

DALORIS: If nothing's hurting you're not dancing hard enough. That's what I say. After class every part of me hurts. I've been doing flamenco about three years now. Take the number two down twice a week. I'm a five year cancer survivor. So I go where the healing is. Flamenco made me love my body again. I lost a breast. Five years ago. For two years I'd see myself in the mirror and cry. Then someone took me to Katarina. It was hard. In class. Even two years after surgery.
(Raises her arm in a graceful flamenco gesture.)
I'd raise up my arm and it'd *pull* the muscles and scar tissue and *remind me* that *the pain was still there.* But . . .
(She claps a flamenco rhythm.)
The first time I heard it? That *heart beat*? I *knew*. It's like when somebody tells you the truth. You know it. When you hear it.
(then)
Flamenco angels, what I've got. My *chicas*. *Mi amigas*. My homies. Me and my girls. I was in a bad situation. In the middle of the dark forest. Didn't think I'd survive. But here I am. In The Circle. The Flamenco Circle. Katarina calls it that. I'm alive and I'm here. I dance for *me* now. Me and my girls. All of us in The Circle come from every which way. Everyone has a story. The road to grace is never straight. But we're walking it. We're dancing. Let Flamenco do its thing. You'll see. Transformation. How you hold yourself. Back straight, shoulders back.

You start walking down the street head high and heart forward. When darkness comes now? What do you think I do? Go to class! I lift my arms strong in the air, throw my shoulders back, stomp the ground, I howl at the moon and I wail at the stars. We're all so *caught up in it*, we forget. The rapture of being alive.

Information on this playwright may be found at www.smithandkraus.com. Click on the AUTHORS tab.

Dramatic
Daloris: Fifties, African American

Daloris is at a dinner party with other middle-aged women from her flamenco class. As the women eat, drink and laugh, Daloris shares memories of her mother.

DALORIS: My mother was from Alabama. She'd soak her chicken in buttermilk and hot sauce for *eight hours* the night before. With season salt, cayenne pepper . . . Oh, yeah! Pancakes in the morning from scratch. I don't know how she found the time or energy. She was a *life force,* my mother, that *blew* through our house, a tornado in motion. Nursing was her passion, *her calling.* Pediatric oncology. When I was a little girl I'd watch her put her makeup on in the morning, brush her hair, go to work. I'd say, "Mommy, how can you be around all those sick kids every day?" She'd reach down to me, put her hand on my cheek, and she'd say, "Sweetheart, if not me, who?" She loved nursing those kids. When one of the kids in her ward had a birthday she'd throw that child a party and dress up in a clown costume herself. She was there at the hospital, it seemed, morning, noon and night—with those children—sometimes I felt—in my little girl heart and mind—that she . . . The only time I saw her rest was at home. She'd read, play her records. And *two other things* took her mind off all the worries of the world for a while. *As the World Turns* and *Search for Tomorrow.* I don't think she really had time to follow them, but— "My stories" she'd call them. "Daloris, fetch me my glasses, honey. My stories are on." I'd curl myself up on her lap like a little lost kitten and she'd be all "Don't be pesterin' me, girl, when my stories is on" and I'd say, "Tell me *your* stories, mommy. When you were a girl" and she'd hold me in her arms and rock back and forth . . . Start talking her Old Times. About Greenville, before The War. Tell me stories about her people, about her mama, her mother's mama, about The Passage and The Crossing, about the deep wind of the Ancestors blowing through me, whispering me their names, I had *spirit history* in me she'd say. Then she'd rock me, stroke my head and . . .

(hums/sings "God Bless the Child")
Them that's got shall get Them that's not shall lose So the Bible said and it still is news Mama may have, Papa may have But God bless the child that's got his own That's got his own

(silence)
All of us have a deep song inside.

Information on this playwright may be found at www.smithandkraus.com. Click on the AUTHORS tab.

Seriocomic
Dorrie: Ten

*Dorrie tells her friend Ada about all her medical problems.
Ada has remarked that Dorrie walks with a slight limp.*

DORRIE: Shoot. I thought I was hiding it. I have early-onset fibromyalgia. I guess I have a lot of problems. Like, irritable bowel syndrome (I had to have a colonoscopy even though I'm only ten, it was sad), and I have insomnia—sometimes I lie in bed all night just waiting to fall asleep and then it never happens and then I just get out of bed and go to school as if everything is fine except I didn't sleep at all the night before, it's scary, and then sometimes I fall asleep in class the next day, it's so embarrassing, and the teacher gets mad at me, she's like, "DORRIE! DON'T FALL ASLEEP IN CLASS!" because she thinks I'm falling asleep because I'm bored but I'm not—I have a medical condition! Also I have a fair amount of psychiatric problems? Like I take Cymbalta, Buspirone and Geodon for depression-slash-anxiety, also I have very mild ADHD I guess but the doctor says I don't need medication for that but I wish I did because I like taking medication, also I pick all the skin off my thumbs because of my anxiety so I have barely any skin on my thumbs wanna see no never mind my mom said I should stop showing people, also I've had fourteen teeth pulled, I had two rows of teeth at one point—when I ate mashed potatoes I had to spit them out 'cause they were so bloody because my mouth was so bloody, and that's it I guess those are all my problems.

Comic
Nan: Mid-late twenties

*Nan and her husband are going through a rough patch
economically. She doesn't make much money and he just
lost his job. To make matters worse, Nan was at a poetry
reading and a thief stole her purse, containing all their
Christmas money. The poet, a nice guy named Allen, found
her purse, and brought it to her at home. When he asks
where her husband is, Nan, not wanting Allen to think that
her husband is a loser, makes this up.*

NAN: My husband? My husband is at work of course. He
works . . . he works for . . . a charitable organization. Like
the Bill and Melinda Gates Foundation, only smaller.
Much smaller. Of course, size isn't everything, it's
the work that matters. And my husband's charity does
very important work, it well . . . well . . . well . . . it digs
wells! His charity drills wells in Africa! It's called All's
Well When It Ends with a Well. It was started by theatre
people. He makes almost . . . nothing, that's why losing all our Christmas money is sort of a blow. We have
this arrangement, one of us has the money job, and the
other one has the repairing the world job. I got stuck
with the money job. The problem is, the money job
doesn't actually make very much. Money. I wish I had
the repair of the world job. When you work at a place
like All's Well When it Ends with a Well, or, say, the Bill
and Melinda Gates Foundation, you work with very
evolved people. You work with people who care about
things, and I bet you can take as long a lunch as you like,
because your long lunches are with *other* people who are
also trying to repair the world, you're working to make
the world better during breakfast, lunch, and dinner, all
the time, you're dedicated instead of driven, or rather,

you're driven in the best way and it doesn't make you crazy or cranky when you come home from work. And it's always clear what's right and what's wrong, even though it's sometimes hard to see the best way to do the good, you are still clear about good. Everyone's fair and kind to each other, and everybody's ideas are given equal consideration. And nobody cares about things like fashion or pro-football or anything trivial, nobody in your office has a face lift or gets Botox. All the paper is recycled effortlessly, the coffee in the coffee room is fair trade organic, and it's always the right temperature without ever turning the heat or air conditioning turning on. It's like a temple, a sacred place. Sometimes, I imagine that I am Melinda Gates. I am wearing a white sari with patterns woven with gold threads in it and I am saving the world from malaria.

(A sweeping gesture with her hand.)

I just wave my hand and poof—the mosquitos are vaporized. I go to a leper colony—I hand out state of the art pharmaceuticals Bill has cooked up in his spare time using a logarithm he found stuck on the bottom of his shoe while running a marathon to cure world wide wall eye. I walk through the streets of Bombay handing out Microsoft word to infant programmers so they can pull their families out of poverty by the age of three. My hair blows in the breeze. I wear no make up but I look refreshed and dewy at all times. I walk through the crowds like a good looking Mother Theresa.

Dramatic
Nan: mid-late Twenties

Nan and her husband Steve had a huge fight about the fake charity they invented—he wants to shut it down, because it's ethically questionable, she wants to keep it going because it's becoming real, and doing good work. At the end of the fight, Steve walked out on her. Nan is terrified that her marriage is over, and she confides in her best friend, Molly.

NAN: *(She gets a new pack of cigarettes out, unwraps it. Lights up.)*
This is my second pack. That's how I know this time it's bad. He's never stayed away a whole pack before. At first I smoked to punish him, because he hated it so much. Then I realized it was because I knew that by the second, or third cigarette, he'd be back. So it was a way to measure the time until he came home. But this time I keep smoking them, and he keeps not coming home, and . . . I just don't understand why he always has to behave a certain way because of some arbitrary rule book about right and wrong. Sometimes you have to bend the rules. I thought we wanted the same things. That we thought the same things were important. Now I walk in the house and I don't know where I am. Our whole life all of a sudden makes no sense.
(She takes a big drag on the cigarette.)
When I was little I went to a fun house called Confusion Hill. It was in this dying amusement park in the hills of Appalachia, everything was made out of fake rotten-looking wood that was so decayed it put real rotten wood to shame. When you stepped into Confusion Hill, everything was wrong. Big things looked small and small things looked big. Shadows were the wrong shade. If you dropped five balls on the floor, they attacked each

other and then rolled away in five different directions at once. And best of all—water ran up hill. That's the thing that had me hypnotized. It was late, my parents were screaming my name, they thought I had fallen off a cliff or something, my sisters and brother were already loaded up in the car. But I wasn't going anywhere. I couldn't stop watching the water cascade into this trough and run uphill. Of course it was just an illusion. Gravity is the fundamental force in the universe. Without it everything we believe to be true just stops. Stops being true, and then, stops being. As long as gravity is stronger than water is, water has to behave. He's too much like water. His relationship with gravity is set. I can't change it.

HOW WATER BEHAVES
Sherry Kramer

Comic
Nan: Late twenties-early thirties

Nan and her husband Steve are having a tough time of it economically (who isn't?). She's obsessed with the Bill and Melinda Gates Foundation, and she is ready to do anything to make her dream of donating money they don't have to save the world come true.

NAN: Let's face it. We're a nation of parvenus. Social climbers. Arrivistas. The problem is that the entire middle class *has* arrived, and it doesn't make us feel as good as we thought it would. Money has not made us happy. Even the one precenters aren't happy. Money doesn't work the way it used to. You walk down the street, can you tell who's one percent and who isn't? No. You can't. No matter how rich you are, you can't have a better iPhone than the guy who serves you at MacDonald's. It doesn't exist. And when it does exist, next month it will come out for 199.9. So you're in the one percent and you have seven luxury vacation homes. But everything you have in those houses is probably in half of the houses of the ninety-nine percent—do you know what this mac, with this much computing power, would have cost if it existed twenty-five years ago? Like 2 million dollars? Now you can get a less elegant iteration for a couple of hundred bucks. You can get better face-lifts when you're rich, and private jets are nice. Bigger diamonds on your fingers, cars that give other cars inferiority complexes. But your life isn't better the way it used to be better, it isn't separate and all gold leafed—you're rubbing elbows with the riff-raff everywhere you go. Everybody has what you have, either the real McCoy or the knockoff version, and if their knock off makes their life better the way your real one does, then what's the difference between you and them

anymore? There's no way to be really rich except phil-
anthropically. That is their Alamo. Their final stand. The
philanthropic buzz of Palm Beach is the last real thing
they had. So of course I wanted to have it.

Seriocomic
Daphne: Thirty

Daphne has been having an affair with her female boss'
fiancée. She meets him at The Natural History Museum to
break things off once and for all.

DAPHNE: It actually wasn't stupid at all. It started out as a
kind of seagull. So it was this bird, okay, and it's flying
over the Indian Ocean or whatever, when it sees this
island. So it swoops down there and there's tons of food
an no enemies or anything so the seagull decides to stay.
For a long time. Like, a long, long time. So long that
by the time the Dutch show up with dogs and rats and
stuff the seagull had plumped up and grown flightless. It
wasn't the least bit frightened of them, see, because why
would it be? It'd never known danger, so it would march
right up to the Dutchmen and their guns. So trusting. So
of course the Dutch think, this bird must be a total mo-
ron, and there you have the dodo. Easy pickings. Still,
it wasn't dumb at all. Not really. Just trusting. No more
dodo. I think there's a metaphor in there somewhere.
Don't call me again, okay? Okay, bye.

Information on this playwright may be found at
www.smithandkraus.com. Click on the AUTHORS tab.

Dramatic
Beth: Thirties to Forties

Beth is in session with her therapist, whom she started visiting after her husband, Alec, was killed in the 9/11 attack; but, as frequently happens in these sessions, she finds herself drifting and talking to us. While she talks to her therapist, this monologue takes place, representing her inner thoughts.

BETH: You know, there are times, if I'm honest about it, I think my husband being killed is the least of my problems. *(Pause)* Well. That came out wrong, didn't it? God, you know, most of my thoughts, as I'm *think*ing them, strike me as perfectly reasonable or at least, you know, well *intentioned*. But the minute I *voice* them . . . Well. Blame the pills. I am currently taking what medical experts call a shitload of medication. Not that my problems are solely chemically based, anyway. I have of course dabbled in the odd anti depressant before. I'm a well educated person living in Manhattan, so, you know, it's considered gauche *not to*. What I've found, though? It's that they, the pills I mean, make everything sort of . . . glazed. Which is not without its perks, I'm here to tell you. Your life coated in Lucite, like a museum exhibit. Visible but free from touch. *(Pause)* Although I have to say, before, before all of this, I was never someone who had her shit completely *together*, but there was a time when my shit was at least all within, you know, *walking* distance. I feel bad. About what I said before, about Alec's death being the least of it. It's not that I'm not overwhelmed by it. I am. I am, in *fact*, utterly . . . capsized. Hence the meds. But. The struggle to, I don't know, to get *through* it, somehow, it eludes me. The point of it. I don't know if that's survivor's guilt or whatever, or any of my other endless nuanced varieties of—you know the Eskimos? How they have umpteen words for snow? This is me with guilt. I'm the Ben & Jerry's of guilt. And when it comes to Alec, I . . . and it's a little monstrous to think that therapy's going to be able to smooth that over. You know? There are some things it *should* be impossible to recover from.

Information on this playwright may be found at www.smithandkraus.com. Click on the AUTHORS tab.

Dramatic
Jessica: Thirties to forties

Jessica her husband Josh, whose outlook on life was radically changed by surviving the 9/11 attacks, have been fighting a losing battle to save their marriage for several years. In this scene, she sits in her mother-in-law's living room on Thanksgiving, drinking wine and arguing with her husband, whom she has finally just realized she has no choice but to divorce.

JESSICA: There's nothing to do, Josh. It's done. We're getting divorced. I *need* to divorce you—it's clear now—to divorce myself from you. What a *mensch* you are. Don't you fucking act like that's not what you want. Like it's not what you've been longing to hear from me for months now so you can go off to the West Bank with a clear conscience. It's not even enough to divorce you any more, it's too late for that even, somehow. You know what you've done to me? You've done it—the exact opposite of what you'd hoped, by the way, so I guess I should take a little consolation in that. For the first time in my life, you've made me wish I weren't Jewish. It's true, I wish I were Catholic, Josh, I do, I pray to a great big blond haired, small nosed Goyish God to make me a Catholic just long enough for me to get an *annulment*. What a wonderful thing that must be. To annul—to erase somebody like that. I'm only telling you the truth. What's in my heart. That's all you've been doing to me, right? You know . . . Josh, I have to tell you . . . and I swore I never would— but in dark little moments, for months now, I've found myself fantasizing what it would be like if you'd been killed with everyone else that day. At first, it was almost subliminal, you know—too ashamed to stay in my mind for long. But then—at some point—and not when you became distant and not when you stopped sleeping with me– not then—only *after* that, only after it became clear that those things were happening not because of what happened to you, but because of who I was, only when you became visibly *contemptuous* of me, of us, only after *that* settled around our apartment like all that grey dust did those first few weeks, that's when I couldn't help wondering what it would've been like if I could have just . . . been allowed to mourn you publicly, once and for all, when the rest of the civilized world was grieving, too. Instead of what I ended up doing—mourning you privately every day since then. It's the opposite of being haunted. Everyone can see you, but I'm the only one who knows you're not there. That everything I loved, your friends and family knew of you, is gone. What I'm saying is, I guess, is for what you've done to us, how you've treated me, you might as well be dead.

Information on this playwright may be found at
www.smithandkraus.com. Click on the AUTHORS tab

Dramatic
Gabby: Nineteen

Gabby has been crying her eyes out in the ladies room because she has just seen her prom date, Peter, kissing another boy. Now she knows why he's different from other boys—and why she loves him.

GABBY: Every day, I see these girls—pretty girls, smart girls, like my friends, my sisters, their friends—all these girls surrounded by these stupid, selfish, asshole boys. I see all of these girls get treated like shit every single day, and just, take it. Day in, day out, just take this bullshit nonsense. And every day it made me more and more determined not to be like that. Me, thinking, "No way that's going to happen to me." Like, absolutely determined not to fall into that stupid boy trap, thinking, no way am I planning my free time and weekends and life around these stupid boys. I have spent a great deal of time avoiding these situations, because I see. I see that it's not permanent, that these guys just run around and try to say the right things and do the right things trying to, whatever, make out or cop a feel or get in your pants and all that. And I'm like, Not Me. No way. *(beat)* And then you. You come along and don't push. You're sweet. You're smart. Funny. You can hold a conversation that's not about video games or sports. You notice when I'm wearing something different. When I get my hair cut or wear it a different way. You like, respect me and treat me nice and . . . God this sounds so stupid. It's so different than anything I've ever seen from anyone else. I have never seen anyone else get treated the way you have treated me. So, I, whatever, let you in? I let you in. And now . . . now I randomly catch you kissing Tommy Miller in the Chem Lab. *(beat)* So you're gay. Whatever. That's fine. I feel stupid that

I was too naïve to catch on before, but okay, whatever. Proms are supposed to be momentous occasions. This has certainly been a momentous occasion. *(beat, she turns to him, direct)* But I have to suspect that you knew about this long before I did. I don't believe that this was some, what, random, freak occurrence. So what was I to you? Huh? Was I, like, some sort of experiment? Some like, barometer for heterosexuality? A human litmus test? And don't try to hide behind some stupid bullshit excuse because if you do I'll come over there and take that stupid flower off your lapel and stab you in the ear with it. Because if you were—and I have to believe that you were because you can't seem to even attempt to placate me with some semblance of an excuse—if you were using me as some test, that makes you slime. Because you knew. And you used me. And that makes you worse than any dumb guy, worse than slime. That makes you shit. *(beat)* So look at me. Look at me and promise me that you weren't using me like that.

Dramatic
Lucy: Seventeen

Lucy is contemplating going "all the way" for the first time, with her boyfriend Greg. She talks about what she thought sex might be like.

LUCY: I guess the thing is—I used to—dream—or daydream or something—that—s-sex was—it was—this was before I got it, before I knew what it actually, yeah. I used to think that you go to this—place—to have It. To do It. And you don't want to go but you have to. You get Sent. And if you're a girl they tie you to a table. Like an operating table. Not tie, bind. Metal handcuffs that come up around your limbs and keep you there. And you're naked and cold and you don't want it but you have to. And then there's this scientist person making sure you're strapped in tight. Then they leave the room but they're watching through a little window in the door like a dentist taking an x-ray. And if you're the girl, you're laying there and the room goes dim. And there's a metal sound from above you. And then the boy descends. He's strapped to the ceiling and the ceiling is coming down on top of you. He's being lowered on top of you. And you're squirming and you don't want it but you're stuck and the scientist is watching through the window and then the boy is on top of you and he's kissing you and you don't want it and he's inside of you and it hurts but you can't do anything about it. Then suddenly, or slowly, you start to like it. You can't help it. You realize you want it and this happens pretty quickly like a hot wave of like a *wanting* and just when you are going to die from wanting to move, the scientist knows that exact moment and from outside the room, he pushes a button, and you are released. The cuffs are gone. The boy is released and you reach for each other and claw at each other and you just DO it and do it and do it and then it's done. And when it's done, the boy is lifted up. You don't even get to say bye. And you are bound again, and then another boy comes and it starts all over again and you're cold and scared. And you look to the window at the Scientist and that's when you realize or guess that it's not a Scientist, it's God or Jesus and he winks at you and it happens all over again. (*Beat*) I'm worried I have—issues . . .

Information on this playwright may be found at www.smithandkraus.com. Click on the AUTHORS tab.

Dramatic
Marjorie: Late forties, African American

*In this direct address to the audience Marjorie, a sickly
alcoholic, sits in her SRO room in Los Angeles and talks
about her philosophy of life.*

MARJORIE: You come in here yourself, you leave by yourself. In between, you alone. And alone get lonely. Officer
Bible Belt ask me why I wanna sit outside when I got a
perfectly good SRO. That boy don't know bread from
a cracker. I'm a homebody, but sometimes even I need
some human give and take. And there's sunshine. I tell
Bible Belt, this LA, baby . . . the sun even shines on a
sleeping dog's ass out here. In the morning, I thank God I
ain't woke up by no police tappin on my shoe. That ain't
no peaceful way to wake up. I like to clean up. I have a
dream of a bigger place to clean, but my dream forgot
to tell my wallet. So you slowly adapt to what you can
afford. You make home. You make home. Wish I had
me a window. Darkness got a way a makin it feel like
time ain't movin. That's why I sit outside. Saint George
community. Strong sense that we all hungerin down
here. I try not to hunger for things I ain't never gonna
get, but it's hard. Hungerin keep you in the abstract . .
. mushy. I think not hungerin allow you to be present,
like a dog present. But I'm a human being. Or at least
I used to be. My bones ache these days and you get the
sense you rottin like a banana on this inside. Maybe
I'm just as crazy as they say. Reality wasn't doin me no
good and them pills was even worse. Sometimes I think
only thing I like in this life is sleep. At least while I'm
sleepin, the bad things don't happen. But I need more'n
just sleep, eat, wander. Someday I get there. Maybe I get

me a little beauty shop and I keep that floor so clean you could eat off it. Hair come in broken, I touch it and it leave fixed. Pretty. Yeah. Somethin like cutting hair got a real special to it. Hair wouldn't grow less it sposeta be cut. God gotta plan for everything. Til then, I just keep on movin. Gotta take care a myself. Ain't no one else gonna. You come in here yourself, you leave by yourself. In between, well, we'll see.

Information on this playwright may be found at www.smithandkraus.com. Click on the AUTHORS tab.

Seriocomic
Shelly: Mid-twenties

Shelly is at a group therapy session, talking about her most recent attempt at dating.

SHELLY: Well, I went out on a date this week. Again. And it did not go well, again. It was a guy I met on the bus. He was attractive, and seemed really into me, and since I've been trying to get better at, you know, sex, still, since Kevin told me how bad I was at it *(tears up)*, so I figured "why not?" when he asked me out. We had a nice dinner, and then went back to his place, and started making out on the couch, and then my panties were off and we were having sex. Well, it started off okay, a little better than before even, since I didn't have to wear a blindfold this time . . . although it did hurt a little, so after a while I just kind of laid there on the couch waiting for it to be over. Once he finished, he said his roommate would be home soon, and I should leave. I asked if he wanted to do something the next night, and he told me that he didn't think so, that he thought maybe I was a bit too . . .

(She's not sure of the word.)

. . . frigid for him—that all the other girls he sleeps with come every time and I told me I should go to a doctor or something. Then he wished me best with my future endeavors and pushed me out the door. So, now I'm zero for sixteen in the sex department.

Dramatic
Lexi: Mid-twenties

Lexi is a graduate student at Yale, going off to her boy-friend's soon to be ex-wife about how she needs to move on with her life.

LEXI: You thought? No you didn't, you don't think, not about him, you think about you though, and about how miserable you are . . . and you don't really do anything to change that . . .you have no desire to climb out of this pit of despair you so enjoy wallowing in . . .but it's been months Emily, and it is time for ALL of us to move on. It is time for you to finally let him be happy. You are an educated, mature woman, why don't you start to take control of your own life, live those feminist values you and the sisterhood fought so hard for and do whatever you can to find your authentic self and embrace the present, become one with it, and merge into this new phase of your life . . . otherwise you're going to become one of those dried up, bitter, bra-burning man haters, who blame all their problems on the younger more beautiful versions of who they used to be.

Dramatic
Stephanie: Teens, Asian American

Stephanie tells Amy, the mother of Luce, a high school classmate, about an upsetting thing that happened to her at a party.

STEPHANIE: There was a party after the last game of the season and me and two friends decided to go. I was drunk. I mean, all three of us were drunk and I don't really drink, so maybe I was too drunk? I don't know. People kept handing out shots of stuff that tasted like bleach and I just kept drinking it because it was easy. I don't drink. I really never do, but eventually I got dizzy and didn't feel well. I lost my friends. I couldn't tell who was who. Frank Orlicki found me and told me to go lie down in the basement. It was really dark. I couldn't see. I felt my way over to the couch but there were maybe three guys there? It could've been more. It felt like more. And in the room, too, I felt like there were more guys, like, along the wall, but they weren't saying anything. No one would let me lie down. I kept telling them I didn't feel well, but they were teasing me and I was confused cause I was still dizzy. And I didn't recognize anyone but it had to be 'cause I was drunk, because I thought I knew everyone at the party. Does that happen? When you're drunk? I couldn't figure it out. Who they were or . . . what . . . exactly was . . . happening. But the next thing I knew someone said we should play the Santa Claus game. This . . . stupid game the guys play where a girl gets passed around from lap to lap and based on how far she lets them go or how much they *like* you sitting on them, they rate you from one to three "Ho, Ho, Ho's". It's one of the easier games. Believe me, there are worse games. Anyway they started passing me around and . . . I tried to kind of play along, but I was really dizzy and didn't feel well. I kept thinking "God . . . what if I throw *up* right now?" And how embarrassing that would be. When they started they were all laughing but the longer it went on—and it felt like it went on forever—all I could hear was breathing. Breathing . . . and counting. 1. 2. 2. 3. 1. 2. At some point I definitely said I wanted them to stop, but maybe it sounded like I was joking? Or maybe it was just something I said in my head. To myself. There were hands . . . everywhere. And sometimes, in their laps I could feel . . .

(She realizes she's crying.)

Anyway. I passed out after that. And when I woke up, Luce was next to me. He said he found them and told them to stop. That he stayed with me all night and he patted me on the head and was like "don't drink so much stupid." I was so . . . happy he was there. Except the next day I went to drop a book off in his locker and a note fell out. It said: "You were right: 2.5".

Information on this playwright may be found at www.smithandkraus.com. Click on the AUTHORS tab.

Dramatic
Mata Hari: Early forties

In the year 1917, Mata Hari, the famous exotic dancer, once the toast of Europe for her daring performances, is locked up in a damp French prison cell, convicted of being a spy for the Germans, awaiting her execution, hoping for a reprieve. From her point of view it has all been a terrible mistake. Lonely in her cell, she has begun talking to herself and to the rats. She is still beautiful, afraid but defiant, and as a poor Dutch girl who has made a good living by inventing an exotic persona and charming men, she still finds it difficult to believe they would actually kill her.

MATA HARI: Sometimes I dream of the Indies. It's pleasant to sit on the veranda in the dry season, but when the rains come, everything is damp. There is mold creeping up the walls, and everything rots. Not unlike this place. In this place the beds are full of vermin, and there are rats everywhere. At first I was terrified of the rats. They disgusted me, and I hated them. But as the days blur one into another I've gotten used to them, even become rather fond of them. They're survivors, like me. I can respect that. Some of these rats possess deeper and more complex souls than many individuals I have encountered in the French judicial system. Look at my judges. Look at that row of pathetic, stern faced, smelly old hypocrites. They look like they've just crawled down off the pictures on cigar boxes. Half of them want to make love to me and the other half think they already have. And they're intercepting my letters. All I want to do is communicate with Vadime. My beautiful Russian lover thinks I've forgotten him. How stupid I was to imagine that any man ever really cared for me. How quickly they abandon me. How cravenly they scuttle away. Not one of them has a rat's testicle's worth of courage. And my poor Russian boy is risking his life at the front for the French government which is determined to kill me. Dearest Marina, he called me. I can't think of him without weeping. What gives them the right to intercept my correspondence? What have I done to make you treat me this way? I have been beautiful, I have given men pleasure, I have danced, and this is my reward. What's that? Is somebody here? Have you brought me something to eat? Have you pardoned me, finally? Am I to be saved after all? Hello? Who's there?

MATA HARI
Don Nigro

Dramatic
Mata Hari: Early forties

*In the year 1917, Mata Hari, the famous exotic dancer,
once the toast of Europe for her daring performances, is
locked up in a damp French prison cell, convicted of being
a spy for the Germans, awaiting her execution, hoping for
a reprieve. From her point of view it has all been a terrible
mistake. She is still beautiful, afraid but defiant, and as a
poor Dutch girl who has made a good living by inventing
an exotic persona and charming men, she still finds it difficult to believe they would actually kill her. On what might
be the last night of her life, she imagines that she has been
visited by her estranged husband, a much older man who
was quite brutal to her. Here she is defending with great
energy and some exasperation what is to her the absurd
accusation that she was a spy for the Germans.*

MATA HARI: I didn't spy for the Germans. I spied for the
French. At least, I tried to spy for the French. The Germans wanted me to spy for them. But I only pretended to
spy for the Germans because that's what the French asked
me to do. And then suddenly the French find my behavior
suspicious because I'm doing exactly what they're paying
me to do. Except they never paid me. I'll tell you how
crazy these people are. The French sent me to Holland
to spy on the Germans. But on the way, I was arrested
in London by the English, who were convinced I was a
mysterious woman named Benedix, who actually was a
spy. When they finally realized I was not anybody named
Benedix, they asked the French what to do with me, and
the French told them not to let me go to Holland, where
they themselves had sent me, because I was a German
spy. So the English sent me to Spain, where the Dutch
consul, who is a Frenchman, tried to recruit me to spy

for Russia. What the hell is the matter with these people? Are all men insane? I admit that I have a restless soul. This is actually considered attractive in a man. Why is it so suspicious in a woman? That's probably why you all want to kill me. Because I can see through you. I can see what you are.

Dramatic
Susannah: Twenties to thirties

*Susannah is sitting around out in the woods with a small
group of people who have survived the recent biological and
nuclear catastrophe which has killed most of the popula-
tion. She tells them about a man who tried to get fuel to
the generator at a nuclear power plant to prevent it from
a meltdown.*

SUSANNAH: He told me that he had gone to do it, he had,
he was at a gas station, a mile and a half from the main
entrance. It's this gorgeous fall day and he's siphoning
off one of the tanks. He has containers. He has a dolly,
or—what are those things, where it's a couple of planks,
basically, on wheels like this
(She indicates dimension.)
and usually it has strips of carpeting on it? He's determined, he's totally set to go. And then he had a, he had
a. A flash? A very vivid—just one of those, fantasies you
have all of a sudden. He said he saw himself walking
towards the plant and there's the reactor right above him,
and up the little service roadway and he's at the shed,
the the the service shed and he busts at the lock until he
busts it open. And he pictures this shed as being, vast,
shadowy, and at the end of it this huge hulking generator. And he steps into the shed and he's maneuvering
the dolly inside when he realizes, that it's quiet. It's so
quiet. He lowers the dolly and he almost can't bear it but
he walks, all the way across the shed, his boots on the
concrete floor. He's standing right in front of the silent
generator and he reaches out, he touches it: it's cold, dead.
He's too late. And his heart is pounding. And he has a
flutter in his stomach which he thought what is this, is
this adrenaline? And he thinks: probably not. And this

ache, starting up in his head. And he leaves the shed and the reactor . . . it's right there, right above him, half lit up by sunlight, And now he gets the first wave of nausea. He discovers he's shitting his pants. And. This is weird. He doesn't want the reactor to get to watch him die. So he starts off, back down the road. And he's thinking, all I want is to get around that curve up there. So I'm out of sight. Feets, just carry me that far. Feets don't fail me now. And this is the point where he snaps out of it. He's standing at the gas station, with his dolly, and, six gas canisters he's scrounged from garages, and a few plastic tubs he found in restaurants. And he looks up the roadway leading to the plant. And he knows he can't do it. He drops the siphon. He walks away. He said: it's not knowing, that's the problem. He said: I think I just can't handle the dread.

Seriocomic

Angie: Late forties to early fifties

Angie, a flight attendant, tells another flight attendant about something that once happened to her.

ANGIE: Do you remember the woman on that Christmas flight, last one off the plane because she was waiting for the wheelchair service to get to the gate? Older woman in the holiday sweater with the snowflakes. And she was so worried about her luggage. She was the one who gave me this bottle of Cognac. After you slipped on the coffee and walked off in a cloud of curse words to the Metrolink, I saw her at baggage claim. Andy was supposed to pick me up but I got a voicemail and he was like . . . "I'm just not going to be home." And so I was going to take a cab home. And the woman in the deep red Snowflake sweater is sitting in her wheelchair. She's at the belt and she's dismissed her handler. She is alone. She is watching a single suitcase go around. And around. And around. And I stand watching this woman watch her bag. She sees me, and she sees my uniform, and she recognizes me from her flight. And she asks, pointing to the bag as it makes its way around, "Can you help me, please?" I pull her bag from the belt. An old, navy blue Samsonite. Too large for whatever was inside. It was so light I almost flung it across baggage claim as I picked it up. And she thought I was so kind to her on the flight and now helping her with her bag, and I said I'm happy to help. And she said she didn't live far from the airport and asked, would I like to come over to her house for a Christmas drink. I didn't want to be alone on Christmas, you know? She makes a call in the cab, calls the nurse who's been at her house caring for her husband. He's a former law professor at

Wash U, dying of pancreatic cancer. She says to the nurse she'll be home shortly and to go home and have a Merry Christmas. Ends the call. I ask, "what were you doing in San Francisco?" to make small talk. She tells me she had just been in San Francisco to visit a friend who knew a man who, it turns out, sells morphine. And to that fact I say . . . "Oh." And I have a very bad feeling, and I want to throw myself out of the cab to get away from this very nice woman. Her home is nice, comfortable. Wreath on the door, tree in the living room. And the woman in the Snowflake sweater asks if I like cognac . . .

(She holds up the bottle.)

Cracks the seal. Pours. We sip. She asks me about what it's like to travel everywhere and do I enjoy my work, and I am afraid to ask her a single question in the 45 minutes we sit in her living room. I give a glance of the watch and say I should be going, and she insists on giving me cash to pay for the cab home. She leaves to get the money. And she's gone for a bit. I think, maybe she's forgotten about me and I should call my cab and go. But she returns with an envelope and she says, "You have been so kind. I would be grateful if you could stay one more hour. Stay downstairs and watch TV if you'd like. I have to take care of my husband upstairs. It would help to know someone was downstairs. To know that someone was in the house with me for the next hour. I probably won't come downstairs. I would 69. Mud Blue Sky 3/19/13 be grateful for your company. Here's some money for your ride home." And in the envelope, there's a thousand dollars, cash. And I said . . . okay. She gets a zip-up leather pouch, about this big, *(gestures the size)* from her very empty navy blue Samsonite, and I pour myself more cognac, and she goes upstairs. An hour passes. I listen to the sound of the house and for any noise upstairs. I'm going to call upstairs for the woman in the snowflake sweater to tell her I'm leaving, and I can't shout her name because I don't know her name. I walk to the top of the stairs and, like. The temperature drops.

The hallway is dark. There's the door to a bedroom at the end of the hallway that's slightly open, yellow light spilling into the hallway. The top of the stairs is as far as I go because I knew—I knew. I didn't need to see it. As long as I didn't look . . . Called a cab. Put the bottle of Cognac in my bag. Let myself out. I went home. Andy had cleared out his closet. I drank the cognac and I drank it until I threw it up and I'm fucking pissed I threw up this very expensive cognac, you know? Even as it was coming out of me I was thinking "this is really expensive vomit." I'm sorry I took her cognac. I put the bottle in the trunk of my car and I was going to return it to her house, but. I should have looked in her room, with her husband, to see. I should have helped or called somebody. I should have done something.

New in the Motherhood
(from *Motherhood Out Loud*)
Lisa Loomer

Comic
Odd Mom: Twenties to thirties

A mom joins some other moms in the park. She's kind of an odd mom out. Not sarcastic . . . a bit bewildered and wry. She's fine with the kid, easy . . . The rest of her new life she's still trying to figure out.

ODD MOM: Oh hi. This bench taken?
> *(Sits)*

Cool.
> *(Sees son, calls out; lightly.)*

Put it down, Harry. Down, babe. The tricycle is a means of *transportation*.
> *(Laughs)*

He's three. Everything's a penis.
> *(She takes out a cigarette.)*

God, I hate the park. If anyone had told me I'd be sentenced to five to ten years in the park . . . I'd have stuck with a cat.
> *(re: cigarette)*

Oh, this is clove by the way.
> *(Takes a drag.)*

All right, it's not clove, but it's the park. See, the park for me is like . . . Dante's Purgatory. Not Dante's Inferno—that'd be exciting, you'd meet interesting people . . . But, I mean, day after day of whose turn is it on the swing? Couldn't we just let 'em duke it out? I mean, I used to go to an office . . . Like—in a building? I was a type A personality! Okay, B minus, but still . . .
> *(Takes a drag; smiles.)*

Look, I know he's a boy, you gotta take 'em outside. They *will not* play Scrabble. They'll throw the pieces at the cat. And they won't miss 'cause they're boys.

(Lightly)

And you can't just let his dad take him to the park, cause, hey—"Where was Mom? Working?" He'll be in therapy the rest of his life—

(Notices; matter of fact.)

Harry? No, honey—put the little girl down. Put her down, babe.

(Waits; easy.)

Put her down and use your words, Harry.

(Beat)

Not *those* words—

(Laughs)

Hey, remind me to cancel Showtime—!

Dramatic
Holly: Thirties

Holly has just learned that she's pregnant but her boyfriend Jacob has too many issues to be able to accept this. Here, she tells him off.

HOLLY: I liked it better when you were trying to manipulate me. At least you had a future. We had a future. It might have been an abortion, it might have been a baby with a father kicking and screaming, but at least he would have been on the ground. Not in some highchair. My womb, your mother's womb. It doesn't matter. You lose 'cause you're lost. You don't take me seriously. You never did, and now I don't care because I see it has nothing to do with me. I'm not even in the room. What's your mother's name? It doesn't matter. Grow up . . . or don't it's no longer my problem. And the baby is no longer yours, I'm really special, you know. Don't agree. JUST SHUT UP. And here's something to know about me. My mother left when I was seven, and my father touched me when I was twelve. So I had five relatively bad years. Big deal . . . There's two ways to look at everything. So remember that. Or forget it. Or something. Just stop. I love you but you're such an idiot. I'll let you know if I'm keeping the baby. Goodbye.

Information on this playwright may be found at
www.smithandkraus.com. Click on the AUTHORS tab.

Comic
Aneesi: Forty-five, Palestinian Muslim

Aneesi tells us about her daughter, Nooha.

ANEESI: My daughter, the middle one, she just get her period. Late start. Nooha, she's fifteen. I get mine when I am eleven. Eleven! Oof. Worst day of my life. Anyway. Tonight we're gonna have fifty people to the house for *Iftar* dinner and she get her period—I say now? In the middle of Ramadan? I need help cooking! She get her period just to get out of helping. I'm serious. My kids is very lazy. Rula, Romi, Nooha—they all sit in the same room on their labtops sending each other messages on the Tweet! Sometimes when one of them leaves the computer on the MyFace, I look at it to see what all my kids doing—we live in Las Vegas! I don't want them to turn into prostitutes and gamblers. But, they good kids and they surprise me, you know? Like, this year Nooha wants to fast for Ramadan with the older kids. So cute. I tell her, no *habibti,* never while you're bleeding. And oh My God, I never seen her so hysterical. She is crying—"I don't want this! I hate this! It makes me dirty." I say, "No! Dis don't make you dirty, maybe make you *crazy.* But dirty, no!" And she say, "Koran says!" I say, No. The Book doesn't mean that. Listen. What is the period? The egg—it is the potential for life. It is . . .eh, how you say . . . the energy of creation. So, the body, she need time to remove this energy that she doesn't need anymore. So, God give time off for the body to rest and the soul to rejuvenate. God is VERY, very smart. Ok? Once a month, a lady she get a mini-vacation. God say, "Listen, go and have a hot bath and eat an ice cream and two pounds chocolate Don't fast, don't pray, don't do nothing but relax." I'm telling you, God, she is a woman.

Information on this playwright may be found at www.smithandkraus.com. Click on the AUTHORS tab.

Dramatic
Iris: Early twenties

Iris, who has autism, tells a young man named Mac who has Asperger's Syndrome how she copes by spending all her time on the internet.

IRIS: That's the beauty of the internet. I don't have to get outside this room to know the world. I have friends online all over the world. I always have someone to chat with. When it's the middle of the night here, it's morning in Europe or when it's early morning here, it's nighttime in Australia. There's always someone online. It's not just chat. I'm an online activist. When celebrities pop up online saying how important it is to cure autism, I start blogging and sending out messages. You know, it's like these people want to take part of my brain—the part that makes me what I am—and cut it out. Cure autism. It's like saying, "Cure your ability to focus deeply," or "Cure your high IQ." What really gets to me is they present themselves as suffering so deeply—the things we go through with our children, these children who are tragically maimed. Then they get into all the cures: Chelation, no vaccines, gluten free diets—My mom could never get it together to do gluten-free. She'd read about it and she'd throw out all the bread, but then she'd discover gluten in some weird place she hadn't realized, like Payday bars, and she'd say the hell with it. It's a difference, not a disability. The internet proved that. All of a sudden these people that everyone thought couldn't talk or were retarded were communicating online and their brains were suddenly revealed. It's like someone in the sixteenth century who had horrible eyesight was given a pair of glasses.

Information on this playwright may be found at
www.smithandkraus.com. Click on the AUTHORS tab.

Seriocomic
Cat: Seventeen

Cat is by herself on a train to New York City. She speaks to fellow travelers. Or perhaps she's making her very own video-blog.

CAT: I work very hard. I get A's in all of my classes. I am on time for everything. For Everything. I work harder than the boys but I don't get rewarded. I hear there was this thing a long time ago called "The Revolution" but my mom doesn't seem to know about it. My mom is always exhausted. Church doesn't help. My mom is on a lot of committees and medication. I think my mom wants my dad to come home. My dad went to see his ex-stepsister in New York and he never came back. I don't know what he's doing there. I mean, ex-stepsister? That's not even a real relation. Plus, she's like, she's not, you know, she's not a Christian. I think she must lead a very scandalous and potentially exciting life even if it does not fall under the contract or rubric or whatever of the Church of God. I went on the Internet this morning and looked up this Polly Freed. I know a lot about her. I am going to get my father back. I am going to bring him home. Mom's in the bedroom with the lights out again and everything's quiet and sometimes, you just have to take matters into your own hands. Do you know what I mean?

Seriocomic
Tammy: Seventeen

Tammy, a student at a Christian high school, has just learned that her parents are going to have another baby.

TAMMY: You don't even know how to work the DVR or the I-pod dock. (*to Mom*) You still read newspapers and you (*to Dad*) wear sweater vests. You have angina. You are such an embarrassment. You are ruining my life. You are too old to have another baby. People are going to think I'm the mother! They're going to think I broke my promise ring and had sex and delivered a secret baby that I conceived with Randy Sanderson on the boat landing at Welcome Arms after curfew. Which we never did! Even though Ashley Ringer thought it was so Christian to stand up at Share Time and challenge my purity. I would never defile my chastity vow. Especially not with Randy Sanderson who doesn't even have underarm hair. We were just talking about Jesus, and the scriptures, and about how gross his bunkmate, Lance, was. He needed to get away from his cabin. Lance smells like warm feet. He's says it's a glandular condition but we don't think so. Randy and I were just talking. And it was nice and all those jerks like Ashley Ringer had to go turn it into something sinful and immoral. And now what are they going to think? They're going to think exactly what they already think. Did you consider even for a second how this baby is going to affect me? You and Dad are so selfish. People talk. Especially people from Lakeside Christian. They talk a lot.

Information on this playwright may be found at
www.smithandkraus.com. Click on the AUTHORS tab.

Dramatic
Kimberly: Forty-six

Kimberly, who has recently had a miscarriage, has had a cancer scare as well.

KIMBERLY: The doctor comes in and says "I don't like this." And I say I don't like it either. This is after the miscarriage which was, you know, really hard. Very sad. And he says: "No. I don't like this mass on your hip. It's hard." And I say "Oh I've had it forever" so he says I have to have a scan in a MRI machine to rule out malignancy. And he leaves and I look at his chart and he has a penciled in C with a question mark. I wasn't able to reach Glen or my sister. It all happened very quickly. And they put me onto this very narrow table and then I was put into a very narrow opening. I was pushed into the machine like at the circus when you put a man into a cannon. Or a coffin. And there was a low hum and I had to stay perfectly still. If I moved even a little bit, I'd have to do it all over again and I just couldn't do that. And I thought about the baby. My child that was scrapped out of me almost ten hours ago and now they're saying I might have cancer. And I know I could handle being sick like my mother was but how would I tell my family? And it's all very much too much. And I prayed just the way my mother taught me to pray when I was a child. And as horrible as my mother could be, I thought about her too. I thought how grateful I was that she taught me how to pray. I asked God to help me find the strength to get through these fifteen minutes without screaming. I am just one person and I don't think I could have gotten through it without God helping me. You really know who you are in moments like this and I have to tell you that I am so grateful that

God was there with me in that horrible cocoon. I could not have survived without Him. I'm fine. It was just a lipoma. A fatty tissue that's benign. I'm okay. We didn't tell anyone about the cancer scare. Jeeze. We think it's hard enough with the baby.

Information on this playwright may be found at www.smithandkraus.com. Click on the AUTHORS tab.

Dramatic
Danita: Early twenties

Danita is doing some sort of penance and has been assigned by a Catholic priest to help out Josh, a sculptor, whose wife is dying of cancer.

DANITA: *(to Audience)* I never understood the expression "heavenly bodies." Because a) they're not bodies. And b) they're not in Heaven. Heaven is a place we can't see. Until we get there. If we get there. If it even exists. Planets aren't bodies, how could they be? They don't breathe. They don't sleep.
  (casting a glance at JOSH)
They don't snore. *(Beat)* They don't move in violent, unpredictable patterns. They're sitting ducks, just waiting for some meteor to strike and shatter them. But they're not bodies. Bodies have hands, and hands are for . . . Do you know what I keep seeing? I keep seeing his hands. I couldn't look at him so I focused on the hands. And the nails, they were . . . They had red stuff underneath. Like dried blood. Not clay, it couldn't have been clay. Clay is for making things. Not tearing them down. *(Pause)* I read there are things out in space called quasars. Nobody really knows what they are. I hadn't heard of them, so I looked it up, and it said: "An extremely remote celestial object, emitting exceptionally large amounts of energy." They look like stars. Scientists think they have black holes inside them, but that maybe they're the beginnings of new galaxies. Imagine, a whole new galaxy in the process of being born. There's hope in that, isn't there? I think that's hope.

SAMARITANS; OR WHERE IS SYLVIA?

Wayne Paul Mattingly

Dramatic
Dizzie: Twenties

Dizzie, an attractive young woman in her twenties, is speaking to Sidney, a chipper gentleman of about seventy. Sidney has left Senior Hollows at four a.m. to take up residence in his old home with his dead wife, Sylvia. The young married woman who now lives there, Dizzie, refuses to allow Sidney inside, and on the backyard patio explains why.

DIZZIE: You know, you can't live here on the patio. It will rain. The season will change. It'll become uninhabitable. You'll become ill from exposure. Or pneumonia. Or some flu. And I don't want to be responsible. Do you hear me?! Do you get it, Sidney?! Hammond and I invent things—we make things up—people, children, events, relatives—whatever we need to keep people out of our lives. Do you know why?! Do you know why, Sidney?! Because we're hanging by a thread. All of us! On the edge of our lives! And the truth is: We don't like people! We're not generous. We're horrible selfish think-only-of-ourselves people. That's our so-called marriage! And . . . oh, Christ, every other marriage I've ever seen becomes a masquerade, a charade in some way because who can possibly sustain all the *interference!* What couple could possibly maintain the solidarity? The lack or absence of bitter contradiction? How? Without enormous illusion and pretense and lies? And here you are. Wedged in. Trying to drive us apart. To destroy us. Not in any way anyone would recognize—oh, no!—except me—me and Hammond—but you are. And you can't . . . you can't stay . . . because it's *insane! Our life is already insane!*

Information on this playwright may be found
at www.smithandkraus.com. Click on the AUTHORS tab.

Dramatic
Deanne: Late twenties

Deanne Sprawley, a recent widow in her late 20s, and her father, Huck Gleason, are summoned to the office of Ms. Henderson to discuss Deanne's son Tommy's behavior in school following the death of his father (and Deanne's husband). Deanne learns that Tommy's behavior in this conservative Christian private school has warranted his suspension from the school. Deanne comes to see that Tommy's struggles with his religious faith (he now questions the existence of God) which mirrors her own, has placed into strong perspective the very definition of religious faith. Are we never to question that which is put in front of us by church elders, or should Christians exercise their God-given brains and tap into their innate capacity for compassion, even when it might be messy and break certain sacrosanct rules? In this epiphanic monologue, Deanne puts all of this into the context of her own life and tragic circumstances.

DEANNE: I used to believe in a lot of things. I have lost my husband, Ms. Henderson. My own faith has been severely tested. Perhaps I've lost that too. Tommy and I—with my father's help—we're just trying to get through each day as it comes. It really sucks, Ms. Henderson. Life sucks. God isn't smiling on Tommy and me right now. I don't blame Tommy for anything he says or does. If he's hurting another child, that's another matter. But questioning the existence of God when circumstances don't give you much of a reason to believe—I don't think that's such an odd thing to be doing. It tells me that Tommy is working his way through this the best he can. And I understand the anger. And I understand the betrayal because I feel it too. But what I *don't* understand is people like *you*, Ms. Henderson. Controlling kinds of people. That's what this school is—I've come to see it now. You control little minds. You put little minds in very tight boxes and punish those who don't stay put. Faith to me has always been a journey of discovery—an exploration. I have never taken anything at face value. My husband taught me to question. We had late night theological arguments. I'm not a stupid woman, Ms. Henderson. But even stupid people still have brains enough to think for themselves and pride enough not to be spoon-fed one particular way of looking at the world.

Dramatic
Juliana: Thirties

Julianna Buchner, the 30-something mother of a young daughter who has been brutally raped by a man whom the criminal justice system has allowed to walk free, has decided to take matters into her own hands by hiring a hit-man to kill her daughter's assailant. When asked by the contract killer in the interview in which the contract is made to murder the rapist, if she will be able to live with herself after he makes the hit, she answers through this monologue—a demonstration of how deeply her revenge obsession has taken hold. At the same time, the monologue speaks to Julianna's aching wish that "none of this should ever have happened." She is tortured, she is painfully regretful, but the overriding emotion is pure hatred, fueled by sudden, fortuitous empowerment. Circumstances have transformed her into a criminal too and she seems almost exultant over this outcome.

JULIANNA: It's all I've thought about since he walked out of that courtroom. I wake up in the middle of the night wanting him dead. I stand in the produce section of Kroger's wanting him dead. I sit at green traffic lights with people blaring their horns and I want him dead. I've never wanted anything so much in my life. Except . . . to be dead myself. But I have to stay alive. I have to nurse Kimmie back to health. I have to be her mommy. There is one other thing. One other thing, Mr. Gampion, that I wish for more. It's an impossible wish: that this should never have happened. That I should have Kimmie back the way it was before. I wish to turn back the clock, Mr. Gampion. But I can't. And I can't go out some night and drive my car off an overpass. So I do the only thing I *can* do: I ask you to end the life of the man who tried to end my daughter's life, and who ended up destroying it nonetheless. That is what I can do. I don't care what God thinks. I don't care what the Bible says. I don't care what compassion requires. I care nothing about any of those things. Kill him, Mr. Gampion. Do it slow or do it quick. Do it however you see fit. And know that I will never change my mind. It won't put Kimmie back the way she was. It won't put Bill and me back the way we were. But I want it done. Now *I* get to be the criminal. Now it's *my* turn. Goodbye Mr. Gampion.

    (She exits. LIGHTS slowly fade out.)

SILA

Chamtal Bilodeau

Dramatic
Leanna: Fifty-three, Inuit

*Leanna, a Canadian climate change activist, has filed a
petition with the Inter-American Council on Human Rights
alleging that unchecked emissions of greenhouse gases from
the U.S. violate Inuit human rights. After her petition is
dismissed, Leanna files an appeal and is invited to defend
her case. Here, she addresses the Council only a few days
after losing her grandson to suicide.*

LEANNA: The issue is not climate change. It's not how warm
or how cold, how much water or how much ice, how many
particles per million, or whether it's man-induced or not.
The issue is not where the tree line will fall, where the
hurricanes will hit, what animal species will make it, and
what islands won't. The issue is not complex or global
or intractable. It's not political or economic. And it's not
even about climate. No. The issue is small and personal
and it has to do with the most inconsequential of things:
human nature. Because who cares about one's desire to
eat their traditional food when millions of others need to
keep theirs cold so it doesn't spoil? Who cares about a
culture having an identity crisis when entire countries are
struggling to lift themselves out of poverty? Who cares
about a nation's love affair with nature when the world's
economic survival is at stake? You and I both know that
upset feelings don't justify the kind of massive disruptions
a grand scale action would entail. You and I both know that
anxiety and fear and depression are a matter of personal
choice, not of environmental stewardship. You and I both
know that drug abuse and . . . teenage suicide . . .
   (a beat as she fights back tears)
. . . are by no means a sign of degradation of the Arctic
but simply an indication of human nature run amok. So

don't be fooled by those who may want to convince you otherwise. The issue is not and will never be climate change. The issue is that we, sensitive humans, are just terribly ill-equipped to deal with loss . . . So it doesn't matter whether the U.S. lowers its emissions or recognizes a violation of human rights. We will always, by default, grieve over what we lose because we don't celebrate what we have.

SKIN AND BONE
Jacqueline Goldfinger

Comic
Emma: Mid-twenties

Emma has arrived at the home of two old ladies named Midge and Madge who operated a bed and breakfast there years ago, where Emma's late mother once stayed. She has been re-arranging the stuff in the house so it looks like it did in the old brochure she found in her mother's things.

EMMA: Why wouldn't you know better what's right in your own home than some stupid little girl? Some little pea brain who don't know her own strength and accidentally breaks a zirconium-studded Princess Diana glassware set that her foster brother was gonna sell on Ebay to pay for the removal of his "I Heart Mom" tattoo because Mom's turned into a real grumpy old bitch, and then her boyfriend dumps her because she accidentally fed his pet rats to his pet snake when he's on a men's retreat in the New Orleans French Quarter with a real sweet girl from his Bible Study Class named Suzy Sucker, and then who goes to work and gets mixed up when people shout at her through the microphone at the McDonald's drive thru so she pushes all the wrong buttons on the register when there's a long five o'clock line and backs traffic up all the way to Route Six so she gets sent to work the milkshake swirl machine but the milkshake swirl machine won't freeze right no more and her boss says it's her fault so they're gonna take repairs out of her pay check so then she's sent to work the French fry fryer but then the grease in the French fry fryer catches fire so she tries to put it out with a bucket of water and when she pours the water on the French fry fryer, the French fry fryer explodes and catches the burger maker on fire and then the burger maker catches the fish-o-fillet press on fire and then the fish-o-fillet press catches the bun toaster on fire and the bun toaster catches the entire McDonald's on fire and it goes up in a big whoosh and the assistant manager's pissed and he's also her landlord so she loses her job and gets kicked from her apartment and so she takes her last $15 and heads out to the only place she knows to go, the last place her momma was, so maybe she'll find something good there. Something good in the last place that anything good ever happened before everything went bad and maybe she can start all over again, Miss Madge. Start something different and keep it good.

Information on this playwright may be found at www.smithandkraus.com. Click on the AUTHORS tab.

Dramatic

Rosa: Twenty-five, Mexican

Rosa is a young Mexican actress, who spends the play in the bathtub in which she was found drowned and possibly murdered. She was starving in New York when taken in by Natasha, a brilliant but troubled director of independent films, and thrust into a central role, that of a girl who drowns in a bathtub. As Detective Mulligan tries to understand what happened to her, we hear her speak and see fragments of her life. In this play death is seen as a kind of dream state in which Rosa can communicate with the other characters as they remember her.

ROSA: I came to New York to study acting. I grew up in foster homes. I had nobody. I wanted a fresh start. I had so many hopes when I got here. But I hated acting school. Acting is this. No, acting is that. This system. No, that system. This teacher is God. No, this teacher is God, that teacher is the Devil. Worship me. No, worship me. They smile and cut your throat. It all seemed so unhealthy to me. I thought if I just got out there and started working, everything would be all right. So I dropped out and began auditioning. But there were so many things they wouldn't even consider me for because of my accent. And my hair. In American culture, there is no such thing as a blond Hispanic girl. So I couldn't get roles because I had a Spanish accent, and I couldn't get Hispanic roles because my hair was the wrong color. So I dyed my hair, but then I was just a girl with dyed hair and an accent. I was running out of money. I wasn't eating. I was just at the edge of the abyss, looking down into the water. I went to a diner, late at night, and ordered some soup. I didn't have enough to pay, but my friend Megan worked there, and usually she'd find a way to get me something to eat. But Megan was off that night, and when the manager realized I didn't have any money, he said he was going to call the police. And I started to cry. And a couple of tables over, there was this beautiful Russian woman, arguing with an Italian woman about something. And she looked over and saw me crying, and how the manager was treating me, and Natasha just jumped right out of her seat, like a lioness defending her cub. She scared the hell out of the manager, bought me dinner, and listened to my story. She was so kind to me. And she said to Emilia, right then and there, "This is her. This is the girl in the tub." I had no idea what she was talking about, and it crossed my mind for a second or two that I'd fallen into the hands of a dangerous lunatic, but I didn't care. She was so wonderful. And they took me in. And gave me a place to stay. And the next day we were shooting the movie. It was all like a dream. Natasha is like a dream.

Emilia: Forty-two, Italian

Emilia is an assistant director, now overshadowed by her beautiful and brilliant director friend Natasha. Here she describes their initial meeting in Berlin, when she found Natasha huddled on a street in the snow, starving and in despair. Emilia rescued her, took her in, brought her onto her movie set, and then gradually watched as the immensely talented Natasha completely took over. Emilia is angry about this, but she remembers her finding of Natasha with great tenderness. She loves her.

EMILIA: I found her in the street, like a stray cat. Berlin was the place to be, if you were a young filmmaker, or any sort of artist. I was walking home late at night from shooting a film in an abandoned building. It was snowing, and I was cold and discouraged, because it wasn't going well, and I didn't know how to fix it. And I saw her sitting at the base of a wall, all huddled up, with her red hair streaming down over her face. I tried to just walk by. You see people in the street. You feel bad for them, but what can you do? You can't help everybody, especially if you have next to nothing yourself. You put your head down and just keep walking. But she seemed so lost, like a creature out of some fairy tale. Of course, in fairy tales a person often lives to regret rescuing such a creature. You bring them home and they end up eating the baby. I thought of the story my grandmother told about her father driving his wagon home one dark night and finding a white bundle at the center of a crossroads, and how he thought it must be an abandoned child, so he stopped and picked up the bundle, but when he saw what it was, he threw it down in the road as hard as he could and drove away. It was a changeling, a demon child. My brain told me to just keep walking, but I found myself turning around and going back. It was one of those moments when you observe yourself doing something without really knowing you were going to do it, but once you're doing it, it seems inevitable, as if somebody else is operating your body. As if your life were a movie, and you're trapped inside the frames. You want to act differently but you can't. So I walked back to her in the snow, and asked her if she was all right. And then she looked up at me, and I saw her eyes. She was so beautiful I couldn't breathe. And her eyes were like nobody else's eyes. Like the eyes of some creature from another world. You're going to freeze to death out here, I said. Don't you have some place to go? Would you like some soup? You need something warm inside you. And so I took the beautiful green eyed stranger home with me, and heated up some soup, and gave her some green tea, and we sat by the fire and talked, and as she warmed up, her face began to glow, and her hair was curling from the moisture in it, and she looked at me like some sad, lost young animal, and my heart went out to her, and I let her spend the night, and we've been together ever since.

Comic
Loli: Twenties

Loli has managed to escape small town life in Flatt, Kansas,
where she was a truck mechanic. Into her tiny apartment in
Los Angeles, covered in blood, bursts a movie star named
Sheena, seeking sanctuary. Sheena hires Loli to be her Per-
sonal Assistant and has renamed her Priscilla, since that's
a requirement for the job, and sent her off to tell her agent,
Galaxy, that Sheena has gone to Abu Dhabi. "Priscilla"
has just returned and tells Sheena what happened.

LOLI: Okay suite one thousand. Now, I went in where you
wait . . . kinda stood on the edge of it 'cause I didn't want
to put my dirty shoes on that Chinese rug. But finally I
just yelled out, "Sheena Keener's gone to Abu Dhabi!"
and boy, all hell brook loose . . . this alarm bell went off,
people whanged out of doors and these vituperous Dachshunds got loose, went after the reception lady. Boy, she
vaulted over her counter thing but she knocked over this
espresso set-up which spilled on this dandy man's white
linen suit and he lets out this yell and his chair tipped
over backwards so his cigar set these skinny curtains on
fire which set off some sprinkler things and then bam!
This young girl with those murderous eyes comes out this
golden door, and all these wet people backed up against
the wall . . . shoot, even the Dachshunds backed up and
she walked up real, real close to me and says, kinda sweet
and poisonous, did I know who Louis the Fourteenth
was? And I did, I studied that. And she said she was the
Louis the Fourteenth of Hollywood, her name being
Galaxy-bigger-than-a-star, So I went into Abu Dhabi real
strong and she asked who it was I figured I was? So I said
I was Priscilla the Seventh, your personal assistant and
she said . . . giving me the death eye ... that if you had

run off she would flay me alive, and she claps her hands and this Dachshund launches at me but I duck and it lands on her, and while the two of them go at it like the lions and the Christians, I ran down seventeen flights of stairs and got me a cab ride back and here I am. Oh, stopped off on the way home and got you a mango.

Dramatic
Reptile Girl: Late teens

Reptile Girl is a carnie performer. Rube Waddell, once a great baseball pitcher but now a has-been who dreams of making it back to the game, has enticed her to his seedy hotel room for a private performance. Here, she talks about her life at the carnival.

REPTILE GIRL: You know I said how I liked it. The show. The ghost show. Getting tied up and looked at. It wasn't power and it wasn't good. That girl who they looked between her legs to see "the secret of the universe." That was me and it killed me. Their hot breath on my thighs. Could smell their hair oil or feel the curl of their beard against me and I'd just shut my eyes, keep my legs open and let them kill me over and over. Dig my nails into the arms of the chair pretending it was their arms, tearing at them. It was mud and shit every day. When some townies didn't get enough they'd come back and take. You wanna lick my scars—that's a big job, you want to get married on roller-skates, you want to pitch and throw. You want to be a steak and a fireman. You want to be everything and I just want to fade away.

Information on this playwright may be found at www.smithandkraus.com. Click on the AUTHORS tab.

Dramatic
Reptile Girl, late teens

Reptile Girl is a carnie performer. Rube Waddell, once a great baseball pitcher but now a has-been who dreams of making it back to the game, has enticed her to his seedy hotel room for a private performance. Here, she talks about her life at the carnival.

REPTILE GIRL: I lost count of my age. Hadn't mattered. When you got no standard schedule—don't really matter how many years gone by. The only real time I counted was when I was pregnant and even then it was only so I could give it up. But I am young and I am beautiful. And my scars are beautiful and my breasts and elbows and all of me. This one fella from New York comes to do the taxes for the circus. He stays for a while. Don't know his name they just call him Yankee or The Jew. His breath was always sour and he was always with a cigarette in his lips. His hair was gone from where he'd wiped his head with frustration. Like this.
   (Demonstrates.)
He was all work. But one night we were somewhere near St. Louis by the river. It was hot and I went down to this place to swim. I swim naked. 'Cause . . . 'cause I feel like a salamander. I like to spread my fingers wide when I swim—feel the water slip through them like I'm letting something escape. I look up and see a glint on the shore. It's the Jew the light was off his glasses. He was just watching me. I swam over and got out of the water. I don't know why, maybe I wanted him to see me or I just wanted to get out or. And I sit next to him on the bank. My body on the grass. He asks me: "Aren't you embarrassed?" I didn't know what he was saying? He says something about how people invented clothes

because of shame. Because being naked scares us. I asked him if I scared him. He said yes. I asked him why. And he just looked out and the night bugs kept on kicking up a racket and he picked up a stone and chucked into the water. He said how many girls must have passed through their youth never being naked and how much that must have hurt them. That in their old age how they must have wished to be sixteen again and run naked. Because back then they were all beautiful even the ugly ones were never more beautiful than when they were young. And I asked him again why I scared him. He took out a cigarette and lit it.

Information on this playwright may be found at www.smithandkraus.com. Click on the AUTHORS tab.

Seriocomic
Semira: Forties

Semira, a very successful event planner, tells Simon, a choreographer/performance/artist, why a foundation is pulling his grant.

SEMIRA: The contract you signed states explicitly that the foundation has the right to pull the grant at its discretion *at any time* based on content of commissioned work. Period, the end. This grant is a gift Babyface, and you blew it. As of now, it's going to someone else. The board thinks you're talented, but your work has simply become too provocative. They made a very reasonable request that you tone things down and you ignored them. This is their response. Last year, you had a circle of men dressed as construction workers holding a wall of barbed wire around a woman wearing nothing but a Vegas showgirl headdress and stilletto heels masturbating. *She was playing with her cootch. (beat)* Call it "reclaiming her womanhood." Call it whatever you want. But, when it comes right down to it, it was twelve minutes of a woman in feathers rubbing her muff to German techno music. If I want to see that, I can turn on Cinemax. Half the audience didn't know what the hell was going on. *(beat)* Look. Simon. I like you. I do. I personally adore the over-the-top theatrics of your work. But sometimes—*most times, actually*—you don't know where to draw the line between art and social statement.

Seriocomic
Stella: Late fifties

Stella, an emergency room nurse is talking to Lou, a bar owner. Stella's about ready for a quieter, saner life than the one she's been living.

STELLA: Yeah, well, I need somethin', Lou. Gotta'... make some changes or, uhh...
(Shrugs)
Maybe I'm just gettin' burnt out—who knows? Like tonight—I hadda' "officially" reprimand one'a my nurses.
(Moves her thumbs indicating texting.)
This all night. Texting. You're on break do whatever you want but we had two gunshot wounds, an overdose and a naked guy who fell three stories into a dumpster—don't ask. Got our hands kinda' full, right, and I can't find her. She's hiding in a closet—I'm not kiddin' Lou. People's lives at stake, literally, and she's on Facebook puttin' up pictures of her cat. Not the first time either so I laid into her. Wrote her up.
(Laughs a bit ruefully.)
Found out what they call me. Give-'em-hell-Stell. Kinda' fits, I guess.
(re: texting)
I swear this stuff is worse'n crack. And I get complaints from patients about how rude some of my nurses are. They're not "rude" they just... they don't know how to talk with actual... people. They can text 'em but they can't talk to 'em. Generations from now nobody'll know how to just sit and have a conversation.
(Mimes texting.)
Babies will be born with carpal tunnel.
(She sighs, tired.)

Maybe I'm gettin' old but it scares the hell outta' me. Seems like there's no real—I don't know—human contact anymore . . .

Seriocomic
Stella: Late, fifties

Stella is an emergency room nurse. She is sitting in Lou's bar, talking to Lou about her unhappiness with her life—in particular, about her disappointment with her son, Charlie.

STELLA: Wellll, Lou . . .
    (She thinks a moment.)
Charlie . . . I love him—he ever needs me for anything I'm here
But . . .
    (Sighs)
If he wasn't my son I'm not sure I'd wanta' sit next to him onna' bus. I know, I know that's awful. Good mothers don't say that stuff but—Lou, if I didn't carry him for nine months I'd swear that Richie had himself cloned. Carbon copy of his father. Oh, and then there's Charlie's wife . . .
    (a beat)
Lou, I don't think I'm a wicked witch mother-in-law. I had one so I always swore I'd never—ya know. But Sage . . .
    (Rolls her eyes.)
Saaaage. What're these parents thinking? That's a spice for God's sake. Anyway Sage is—what's the right word? Coarse. Sage is coarse. Never met a sentence she couldn't squeeze a couple profanities into. Wears a necklace looks like somethin' you'd put on a doberman. And tattoos—okay, they all have tattoos nowadays but she's like somethin' out of a circus.
    (Indicates her arms.)
Sleeves. I'm not kiddin'. That's what they call it. Her neck. I don't even wanta' think about where else. Every

time I look at her I think "hepatitis." And ya know, Lou, I could overlook all that—I could!—if she was just . . . nice. She is not a nice person. Not a kind bone in her body. I stopped goin' over. I just don't feel welcome. Now they're talkin' about havin' a baby—she smokes like a chimney by the—way—and I'm thinking, "Please, no." I'm tempted to sneak birth control pills into her tequilla.

Dramatic
Emma: Forties

Stupid Fucking Bird *is a contemporary version of Chekhov's*
The Seagull. *Emma is the Arkadina character, a famous*
actress. This is direct address to the audience.

EMMA: When he was little I used to make my hand die.
(Pause) He'd be . . . screaming or whatever . . . and if he
wouldn't stop, I'd tell him he was hurting me. I'd tell him
. . . I'd tell him he was killing me, actually, that's what
I said, I said "You don't want to kill mommy, do you?"
and then I'd . . . make my hand die. Like this . . .
(She makes one hand slowly, sadly, wither and die.)
And he'd get this little look on his face . . . and he'd
stop. It was very *effective*. *(Pause)* I can't help but think
now that that was not, perhaps, perfect parenting. But it
worked... And I needed things—*anything*—that worked
(Pause). I was 18 when I got married. Eighteen fucking
years old. Hardly out of diapers. To my first famous leading man. Dixon. Dixon McCready, remember him? No,
me neither... Jesus, the way he said his own name should
have tipped me off . . . "Dixon." "Dixon McCready.
Rhymes with seedy." Oy . . . "Sexual harassment that
just worked out" we called it. I thought that was so funny
and charming at the time. Like we'd beat the system.
What did all those "adults" who thought they knew better,
that told us to wait, that told me I was too young, what
did they know? I *knew*. It was true love! It was perfect.
"What could possibly go wrong?" I asked my mother
during one of our stupid, endless fights. *(Pause)* "What
could possibly go wrong?" *(Pause)* Well, as it turned
out . . . *things. Many things* could go wrong . . . And did.
Wonderfully, impossibly wrong, and at 22 I had my first
hit movie, my first tabloid scandal and I was a divorced

mother of a two year old son. *(Pause)* And the universe said . . . "Well, good luck with *that.*" *(Pause)* So, yes, that's right, my point is, indeed, don't judge. Don't you dare judge me. *(Pause)* You've done it all perfectly, have you? Love. Life. Career. Family. Fidelity. Passion. All right then, all you . . . socially responsible, deeply fulfilled, vegan, charitable, millionaires . . . who work out and have sex three times a week . . . *you* can judge. The rest of you . . . *shut up.* I'm doing the best I can *(Pause)* I don't hate him. How could I? I don't hate him. *(Pause)* But he does . . . *bother me.*

Dramatic
Nina: Late twenties, African American

Nina, a hustler and drug dealer, has been confronted by her father, a former radical political activist who has done a long stretch in prison, whom she grew up never knowing. He's just gotten out and wants to reconnect with her, and wants some letters she may have written to him by her mother, also a radical activist, who descended into drug addiction and, eventually death. Nina bitterly resents her father and all he stands for.

NINA: I don't give a fuck about your fight. Fuck your progress! This is your progress, nigga. Me. Here! I'm your fuckin' progress. This is what you achieved. Shit. Deal with that, nigga. Deal with the sacrificial fuckin' lamb to your better world. And what is better, hunh? What the fuck did you achieve? My mama died with a broken heart waitin' on your progress. You were the muhfucka who wouldn't throw her a damn bone. You want these letters so bad? Why'd you never write her? I'm not talking about them scrap pages of your ideas and meditations while you were locked up and gettin' your brain swollen with information on politics and philosphies and whatever. I'm not talking about your intellectual masturbation on a fuckin' piece of prison paper. I'm talking reciprocity. I'm talking speaking from the core of your gotdamn heart instead soundin' like a fuckin' activist robot. I know her better than you ever will. I listened to her pine over your worthless ass. Listened to her talk about what she thought made you such a gotdamn hero. How you stood up for niggas gettin' railroaded by the justice system, how you stood up for anybody being brutalized by the cops, how you protested corporations helping to fund apartheid, how you did all this shit for the whole gotdamn free world. But when she told you she loved you, what you do hunh? When she told you she wanted you to settle the fuck down and be with her, what you do, hunh? You stand up for that shit?

Dramatic
Zelda: Mid-twenties

Zelda Fitzgerald tells her husband Scott that she thinks she may be going crazy.

ZELDA: The mania . . . what I feel when we're at a party, when I lift up my skirt and dance, when we do something crazy . . . it's gone. What's wrong is I'm seeing that this is what's underneath . . .

> *(beat)*

I used to think this feeling, this . . . vacancy inside me, that it was just a slip, that I had gone under but at any moment I could break the surface again. But what if this is it? What if this is lucidity? What if this is when I'm seeing things clearly and it's the other me who's the fake, who doesn't really exist? I don't know if I can bear it! I thought if I laughed enough, and danced enough, and was gay enough that I'd be safe . . . that it would skip me some-how. I don't know why I thought we could escape it—I don't why I thought—I—I don't know *what* I thought . . . Oh Scott! Am I cracking up? I don't want to lose my mind, I don't . . .

Oh Goofo, you're my one true jelly bean, you really are! *(pause)* And I'm your Sally . . . for I am a salamander, the mythical Salamander that can walk through flames and emerge unscathed . . . as long as I have you.

Information on this playwright may be found at
www.smithandkraus.com. Click on the AUTHORS tab.

Dramatic
Janine: Early to mid-twenties

Janine was to have been married today, but her fiancé drowned in the Mediterranean just days before. Despairing, her plan to follow him into the sea and join him has hit a snag: she's pregnant. Uncertain as to how to proceed, she encounters a stranger (Derek, who lost his own significant other a year ago and had the same idea) and enlists his help in trying to figure things out.

JANINE: He asked me to go with him. Just on the boat. Jerry said it would be a great way for me to overcome my fear of the water. And I promised I would do it. I went to the pier, put on my life vest . . . I even got in. Then the boat rocked and I got right back out. Lucky me.

(Beat)

The only reason I'm still alive, that I'm still here is that I broke a promise to the one person I swore I would never break a promise to. And now he's dead... and I'm a ghost. I'm supposed to be down there with him and if I'm supposed to be there, then . . . And all I am asking for . . . all I want is one measly sign, some indication . . . I'm not looking for a sign from God! I'm looking for a sign from . . .

(Beat)

Look, all I want to do is stand there, and . . . and I'll wait for him to tell me what to do... if he wants me to stay out here and do this all by myself, which I don't think I can . . . Or if he wants us . . . That way, we can all be together. But either way, I just want one day . . . this day . . . to feel like he has his arms around me, holding me, telling me that one way or the other everything's going to be all right.

Dramatic
Sydney: Eighteen

Sydney snuck onto her boyfriend's computer and read a play he wrote about an act of violence on campus. The boy's mother mistakenly thinks he failed out of college, when in fact he was kicked out because of the perceived threat. Sydney confronts the mother to tell her the truth.

SYDNEY: It was his play. He was writing it on his own, like instead of doing homework and stuff. And for like the whole semester it was all he worked on. But he wouldn't let me read it, or even talk about it. He was obsessed with this play and I wanted to know why. To see in his head. Sometimes he just gets so quiet, you know? So we were in his room one time and he went to take a shower. And I knew I had like fifteen minutes at least, so I got on his computer . . . and I know I shouldn't, it wasn't my business . . . but I emailed it to myself. So that night I read his play. And it scared me. You know Jacob. I mean he gets angry . . . you know, moody, pissy sometimes. But this play . . . his play. It was just different. Violent. Really violent. About school. And it just seemed so personal. I mean, I think everything people write is personal, but this seemed like it was more than that. I had this feeling . . . you know? You hear stories. On the news. When bad things happen. And everybody says they didn't know. I mean, maybe they thought the guy was acting kind of strange, but they didn't really know. Not what the guy would do at least. Like with that Congresswoman in Arizona. Or Virginia Tech. But what if they did? What if they knew but they just didn't want to know? I'm probably totally wrong. I didn't know what to do though. So I told my adviser. I gave her the play. I didn't know they were going to kick him out. I swear. I wanted them to help him. Why didn't they help him?

Dramatic
Nadine, early thirties

Nadine's husband, Tyrone, is heavyweight boxing champion of the world. She has just learned that her husband has been having an affair with a 17 year-old girl named Betty, who wants to atone. Nadine lays into her.

NADINE: I don't want *atonement,* or any other damn thing from you, girl. Except . . . except I want you to know this.
   (She takes a big breath.)
Sometime you want something so badly, you got to make a big sacrifice so you can get it. You say to God, "Please give me this thing—this thing that make me feel like I got a reason to be alive." And in return, I do what I have to do so I can keep it. Now that something—if it's a marriage, a baby, a love that stirs up things you didn't even know you had in you—it don't matter to you if that something is right or wrong or good or bad for you—and I don't think it matters much to God either. 'Cause you got a free will, don'tchu? You ask and pray and hope and cry for this one thing until one day, low and behold, you got it. You got your reason to be alive and you're so filled with joy at first that nobody can getchu down about nothin.' *(Pause)* But then . . . then it come time to make that sacrifice you agreed to make. You gotta pay up. Cause big Old Man Happiness—huh! He ain't cheap, I'll tell you that. So you pay and you pay and you pay until you wake up in your bed one morning, in the life you always wanted and you realize you done gave so much to Happiness that that tricky old bastard don't live in your house no more. And maybe ... maybe he never did to begin with. *(Pause)* Sometime what's real

ain't nothin' but whatchu believe in. Sometime you're asleep until someone shakes you awake and shows you whatchu been lyin' to yourself about. *(Pause)* Now I think we can agree on one point here, you and me. The two of us together—we been sleep-walking for some time now. And that just can't go on any longer.

Information on this playwright may be found
at www.smithandkraus.com. Click on the AUTHORS tab.

Seriocomic
Eliza: Thirties

Eliza is a computer genius, intent on developing a system which will top IBM's Watson, which recently beat the three greatest "Jeopardy" champions. She is talking to a computer techie who works for the Dweeb Squad, whose name happens to be Watson.

ELIZA: I'm actually just starting out on my own right now, so this is all still in the dream phase for the most part, but I'm developing a device that will support deep Q&A and also be highly sociable, so like, it'll answer any questions you have but it'll also ask you questions of its own, you know, in response to your emotional cues. The core of the technology is based on IBM's Watson, I don't know if you heard about the supercomputer that beat the humans on Jeopardy a few weeks ago? I was with Watson in the beginning. But then I left. And my system is going to be really different—it won't just be a super-enhanced trivia machine. I'm working on a prototype for a low-cost, high-performance companion unit that will act as a personal advocate for people at the fringes of society. Like low-income people, nursing home patients, disabled vets. These people have been betrayed and abandoned over and over again by the very public institutions that are supposed to serve them. They need reliable, highly skilled, personalized support, a device that can get to know them better and better as it helps them navigate the social services system. So like, you're poor, you need to go on public assistance. Instead of dragging yourself down to HRA and standing in a dehumanizing line for five hours and getting turned down anyway because you didn't fill out the stupid form right, you activate your companion device before you even leave the house. He retrieves all your documents, analyzes and leverages complex background information for you, and then, because he's fully socially enabled, entertains you if you *do* have to stand in line, and reassures you when he senses that you're distressed. The potential applications are—I mean, unfortunately—endless. People are just plummeting through the holes in the safety net, you know, all over the country, they're literally *dying* for care, and there just isn't the manpower to meet their needs. But with my device, that can all change. And of course, social justice is not exactly sexy to multinational corporations. That's why I had to strike out on my own. I want *actual* better living through technology, you know?

Information on this playwright may be found
at www.smithandkraus.com. Click on the AUTHORS tab.

THE CURIOUS CASE OF THE WATSON INTELLIGENCE
Madeleine George

Seriocomic
Eliza: Thirties

Eliza is a computer genius who has plans to develop a system far superior to IBM's Watson, which beat the three "Jeopardy" champions. Here, she is having a conversation with Watson (the computer), about her recently torrid love affair with a computer technician from the Dweeb Squad— whose name is Watson.

ELIZA: Anyway it's not just the sex. It's that . . . this guy *knows* me. And his learning curve is insane, I mean, I've only been with him a few times and he already knows things about me I didn't even know about myself. Like, the third time he came over he brought me an LED color changing showerhead, I don't know if you're familiar with the technology? You screw it in and it turns your shower into a wet and wild disco, or that's how he described it when he was standing there in my bathtub installing it without even asking my permission. It's actually a pretty ingenious little piece of engineering, and it turns out you can have a pretty great time in there if you turn off the lights and—anyway the *point* is, this is not an item I would ever, ever have brought into my home, and how did he *know?* That I would actually *love* a wet and wild disco shower? It's some kind of crazy predictive algorithm he's running—not just mirroring, it's enhanced, somehow. It's way more sophisticated than anything you can do, buddy, no offense. He always knows what I want. Half the time he gives it to me before I even ask. And he genuinely doesn't seem to want anything in return. With Frank, everything he ever did for me was just the opening move of some calculating transaction. This guy is . . . I would have to describe him as *preternaturally* chill. Purely, perfectly self-contained. I mean, I don't understand the mechanism. I can't begin to guess how he actually came about. And I know it sounds too I-Robot-y to be real, but I honestly can't think of any other rational explanation for what's going on. There's no way I could feel this way about a normal human guy. And you know what they say: when you have eliminated the impossible, whatever remains, however improbable, must be the truth.

Information on this playwright may be found at www.smithandkraus.com. Click on the AUTHORS tab.

THE FARM
Walt McGough

Dramatic
Parker: twenties to thirties, African American.

A new operative at the CIA, Parker has been charged with interviewing a retiring agent, and discovering what went wrong on his final mission. The agent is not cooperating.

PARKER: Let me explain something to you. The Farm is for convalescence. The Farm is the finish line. The Farm is really fucking far away from you right now, because you've spent the last twenty-four years maintaining the ability and willingness to kill anyone you encounter, and that's a very useful thing for field work, but not for a retiree, no matter how much government-funded beer he drinks at some resort. Does that make sense? You are not unique. You are not special. You are a tool, that was mass-produced two decades ago to be a very specific way, and all of a sudden you decided you didn't want to be a tool anymore, and you walked away from it, and that decision happened to come shortly after a mission that you pretty much have to agree went to fuckshit with no warning. There are a lot of red flags there. I've read your resignation, and I've watched the debriefings, all of them, and I've heard all the song-and-dance about "the way things was," and the only thing that I have gotten out of all that is the impression that you are a man who is trained to lie to people, and you are incredibly good at your job. And, you are using all of your considerable faculties in that department to pretend to be balanced, and stable, and ready for re-entry into society. I don't buy it. Something went wrong, something that you're trying to keep down, and you think it's okay and that you can just keep it inside and go into the real world with it, but it's not okay because you don't know how the real world works anymore, and you haven't for two decades. And that means that I am going to keep you in this goddamn room until you've convinced me that you're not going to flip out at a Costco and choke a toddler because you think that he's wearing a wire. Once I'm satisfied, you can go to the Farm, but the burden of proof is on you.

Information on this playwright may be found at www.smithandkraus.com. Click on the AUTHORS tab

Dramatic
Parker: Twenties to thirties, African American.

Parker is a new operative at the CIA, having come to Langley after dropping out of training to be a Secret Service agent. After being goaded by the agent she is interrogating, she explains why she decided to change jobs.

PARKER: I didn't get fired from the Service. I quit.
(*Beat*)
You heard of the dead man's twenty seconds? It's the amount of time you have to live, on average, if get shot in the femoral artery. If you're in the service, if you're training, like I was, then your instructors all tell you to spend that time shooting. Because you have something bigger than you to protect. You have the President. And he's your life. If someone runs at him, you step in the way. If the plane's crashing, you give him your chute. If anything goes wrong, you always know just where he is. Always, always, always. And if a firefight starts, and you take one in the leg? Twenty seconds. Keep on shooting. Protect him. You spend whatever time you have left getting out in front, and when you're finally dead they use your body as a shield. I never really got that. It didn't . . . I don't know. Click. I aced all of the tests, I hit whoever I had to, I was fit, but when the time came down to it, and it was the package or me, I . . . hesitated. I got a lot of fake presidents killed. And I felt like I was failing. Like I was a bad soldier, whatever. So one day, I finally have a break, and I go out for a walk. And it's cold, it's icy, and coming towards me, there's this woman. She's pregnant. Fifty feet in front of me, her stomach is...she must have twins, or triplets, she is *huge*. And she's coming towards me, and all of a sudden, she slips. Hits an ice patch, and just goes down, face first. And

I'm too far away, I can't stop her, but she...she throws out her arms, right out in front, and she's falling *hard*. And she throws out her arms, and her hands hit the ground, right on her palms, and she pivots a little, and crumples. I get over to her. She's on her side. I roll her over, and I look down at her hands, and her wrists are both broken. Compound fractures. And her hands hanging there, her arms are both limp, and she's looking at me, saying, "Oh my God, I hurt the baby." Over and over. Now, she didn't. Hurt the baby. Her stomach never touched, she caught herself, with her hands, and then rolled, but she . . . I call an ambulance, and stay with her the whole time, and all she talks about is this baby, how she's scared that she hurt it when she obviously didn't. All she says. And that's what they want you to do, in the Service, and I don't have it. Whatever it is, that makes you throw out your hands? I can't see myself doing that for something *inside* of me, let alone . . . So I quit. And my instructor recommended me to Wilcox. Said they were recruiting, big time, and they could probably use someone like me. Whatever that meant. And so I went, and joined up, and then in training I read all your files, and I thought, well, yeah. Maybe. They could probably use someone like me. So? Did I tell the truth?

Information on this playwright may be found
at www.smithandkraus.com. Click on the AUTHORS tab.

Dramatic
Lily: Forties

Lily is speaking to Janet, a dowdy, divorced high school teacher and her best friend whom she hasn't seen in a while, exhorting her to join her in an adventure—anything to get out of the rut into which her life has fallen

LILY: What I've, um, taken to doing, in that big old house mansion of mine is, we get a new bed, every couple months or so it seems, we get one with water then foam then better foam then a remote control, but I don't sleep in them. I've taken to sleeping in a box. On the floor. I've got a box on the floor, and every night I lie down in it cross my arms, and have one of our gardeners stand over it. As I fall asleep, he starts to shovel dirt on top of me. Shovel full. After shovel full. Of cold dirt. Shovel full. After shovel full. Of ice, cold dirt. Spreading across my face, my chest, filling up the box around me, just slowly sinking into this cold, dry dirt. Every night. But. But, I only have him fill it half way. And in the morning, it is so easy to get out of. I just stand right up and leave all the dirt behind me, clumps of it drop right off and fall to the floor. One day that box is going to be all the way full, and you can't get up out of that, but now, right now, it is so easy to get out of. That's what half-way means. The best thing that's ever happened to us is gonna stay the best thing? Why would we even consider not going! Not New Orleans, fine, fuck it, somewhere else, some beach someplace, seafood and tequila and sand all day after day, but it is insane not to do that, it is insane to stay here in suburban fuckin' New Jersey instead. What could stop you? I know what you're gonna say, your kids, and then I know what I'm gonna say! Bring em! We'll call em different names. Of course they didn't want to live in the hovel and be baby-sat by the Queen, but go someplace wonderful and they'll want to come too, and we can raise them together like some beautiful lesbian couple.

Information on this playwright may be found at www.smithandkraus.com. Click on the AUTHORS tab.

Dramatic
Lily: Forties

Lily is speaking to Janet, a dowdy, divorced high school teacher and her best friend whom she hasn't seen in a while. Janet has gotten I into trouble when she made a video mock-threatening her family which went viral all over the internet. Lily wants to help Janet get out of the rut into which her life has fallen.

LILY: Do you have a copy of the freak-the-fuck-out video? Can we, uh, do you think maybe, if you want to . . . C'mon! How many times have you watched me freak the fuck out, and the one time you do it there's video evidence and you won't let me watch?! I bet it's so funny. Now that time has passed, I bet it's become funny. "Shane, if you don't want blood all over your poster board I'd get to that science fair . . ." "Trevor, if you don't put away those socks you won't have feet to put em' on, Shane, let's see you work that smartphone with severed fingers you son of a bitch!" Oh. That was all cheering up stuff. Right there. Y'know what? Let's not watch it. More time, more time can pass. Then it'll be funny. Janet. C'mon. Oh. Do you know what's funny now? I've got something that's funny now. You'll like this.
(Grabs the Jaguar mirror.)
Here's one. I've got a good one for you. Didn't knock this off parking, not at all. I was driving that fancy vintage car, flooring it cause that's what you do, and I just sideswipe, length wise, this parked car, side-swipe the whole thing and there's a sound like you wouldn't believe, metal and glass scraping and crashing, and I just, fucking loved it, like adrenaline, and thought, yes, let's do this, I just nail the gas down and twist the wheel and then I slam into this other car across the street and keep

the gas down, turn the wheel, and keep ping-ponging, zig-zagging down the street, pedal to the metal, (like a what's one of those, pinball machines?), crashing and smashing car after car after car till I'm all sideways and half rolled over, shattered glass and busted tires. I get out and it was this like still, cool, quiet night, and I was like, "what have I been doing all these years?" This, this is what I should've been up to. It was so fucking *real. (Beat)* I didn't side-swipe that first car on purpose, but after I did, it felt so good I wanted to do it again. And again. Actually, you know what? Now that I think about it I did side-swipe that first car on purpose. I totally made the decision to hit that first car.

Information on this playwright may be found at www.smithandkraus.com. Click on the AUTHORS tab.

Seriocomic
Tam: Thirty-two

Tam is a fifth grade teacher at an inner-city "at risk" school. We wouldn't call her a fag hag . . . not to her face. She's an organizer, a do-er, a shaker, and she can drink you under the table. She tells Evan, a gay friend, about one of her students.

TAM: He's not gay, just artistic. I don't have any gay kids this year. At least not that I can tell. I hear all these stories about how kids are starting to come out younger and younger. But, not at my school. My kids learn to put on their tough faces so early. I don't know what the hell happened to childhood, but it's almost extinct in the public school system. They all want to be manly, even the girls. And they all want to be rappers or football players, and I'm supposed to tell them that's a viable career path because it would be classist or racist of me to steer them toward something potentially culturally shaming like—oh—dentistry. I just wish I could actually say some of the horrible things that I'm thinking. But ... the *last* thing these kids need is another white authority figure telling them what to do. I quit teaching at the college level because I could no longer tolerate all that effing white privilege, all those self-important, self-entitled bags of wonder bread telling me that I needed to do something about their grades because they were paying good money for their "education." So I walked away from a perfectly promising tenure track so I could spend every day slapping band aids on these poor kids. Literally, they're *poor* kids, Evan, they live in projects. And they come to school and listen to me say "Do this. Don't do that. Learn this white person's name. Pronounce all the syllables in this word. Don't forget to tuck in your uniform." But it doesn't matter what subject I'm teaching. The only thing I'm telling them over and over is "I can make you better than your parents. Listen to me and I will *make you better*." I've become that self-righteous bag of wonder bread. Only now I'm older, and single, and broke. Cheers.

Information on this playwright may be found at www.smithandkraus.com. Click on the AUTHORS tab.

THE JACKSONIAN
Beth Henley

Dramatic
Eva: Thirties to forties

It is 1964. Eva is a barmaid at the Jacksonian motel in Jackson, MS. She is talking to Rosy, a teen whose father has been staying at the motel since he and Rosy's mother separated. Eva has her sights set on Rosy's father—particularly as Fred, the bartender, has told her he won't marry her. A black man has been convicted of a murder and Eva knows that, in fact, Fred did it.

EVA: Your daddy's cute. Always so well groomed. Thing is the nigger's old and blind. Could die in the jail if they don't gas him fast. The law has got to stop monkeying around. Murder happened back in April. Now some Yankee's coming down here making appeals to the court. Got the law out hunting new evidence. Running out investigating innocent white people out of prejudice, pure prejudice 'cause they sick of having all them coloreds filling up the jail. Want some white suspects for a change. Fred ought to be clear of all suspicion. He has an alibi. An airtight alibi. They came inquiring about his whereabouts concerning the night the cashier woman got robbed and killed. Some passerby saw a car looked like Fred's driving off after shots was heard. Got three numbers off the license plate that matched Fred's. Which was nothing but circumstantial coincident. Fred let them know he was nowhere near that situation. He was with me, his fiancée and no one else. I swore to them it was all the truth. They took me in for questioning. Deposited me in front of a whole line of fancy rich men in suits with their secretaries. I had to tell the truth about me and Fred, what we were doing that night the cashier got shot. All of it was none of their business. It involved sexual relations. You might not know about that. They didn't spare my modesty in any way. Everything. Every detail. Even told them that after the sexual relations I got up and went to the bathroom to douche out the seed. Did it three times for safety. I didn't like revealing that private information. I wanted people to believe I was a virgin. Pure and unsoiled till my wedding day. But the truth is the truth and God will forgive me. Every Sunday I ask Jesus to forgive me. Forgive me, Jesus, for every breath I take. He has to do it—forgive me. That's all He was born for. Every Sunday I get His forgiveness. Regular, like a bowel movement. In the end they will execute that nigger in a gas chamber. All alone but with spectators. I'd like to see it. I'd look at him with pity. Christian pity. It wouldn't be hate.

Information on this playwright may be found at www.smithandkraus.com. Click on the AUTHORS tab.

THE LAST SEDER
Jennifer Maisel

Comic
Michelle: Late twenties to early thirties

*Fed up with her family's constant carping about her failure
to bring a significant other to their annual Seder, Michelle
approaches a total stranger and asks him if he will be her
date this year. This is the "Last Seder" because the family
patriarch is dying.*

MICHELLE: Ummm, excuse me—hi?—look, I know you don't
know me, but you look like someone who might . . . might
be open to a complete stranger asking you . . . I'm not some
psychochick, in case you're thinking I am which I'm sure
you are—here's my license, so you know I'm me . . .
(She hands him card after card from her wallet.)
Here . . . Library card, museum membership, prescription
card—so at least you know I'm a semi-cultured liter-
ate insured psycho, I guess. Thank you for not running
away. It's just that for months I've known this was coming, there's been this impending dread which was only
exacerbated by the Hallmark store across from me—its
windows a mad succession of hoblins goblins witches
and candy accented by Happy Jewish New Year and
Day of Atonement cards and Halloween wasn't even
over before they added Indians and Pilgrims decorat-
ing Christmas trees sprouting out of Plymouth Rock,
of which I doubt the historical accuracy, and then Val-
entine's Day, hearts everywhere since New Year's and
now they have Easter Barbie, Easter Barbie for Christ's
sake which really gets me up in arms even though I'm
not religious. Really, it's more of a cultural thing I have
to admit, but all they'd have to do is stick a jar of gefilte
fish and a Haggadah in the leftover Easter Barbie's hands
and we'd make all the little girls with mezuzzahs on
their Malibu dream houses very *(She catches herself in*

the rant.) happy . . . Right. Well . . . every day . . . every day some relative calls me to confirm whether I'm bringing flourless chocolate cake this year to seder—with my family Passover is a big hulabaloo—not so much in a do everything-according-to-the rules sense but more in a digging-horribly-and-obsessively-into-every-detail-of-your-life-between-appetizers-and desserts sense—and since it's the last time . . . well . . . it's all much more . . . that. But they're really not calling to find out what I'm bringing, but who I'm bringing and I couldn't put up with hearing Aunt Mabel say, "So Michelle, why don't you have a man yet?" in her frog voice. Again. I'm tired of making excuses and I'm tired of sympathetic "I've-got-a-friend"'s. And this, this is the last year so it becomes important in a way I can't explain. So I'm walking up to you, and you must think I'm crazy and I know you don't know me but you're wearing a nice suit and you looked somehow . . . right . . . and that's a step in the right direction anyhow. Do you like matzah?

The Sins of Rebethany Chastain
Daniel Guyton

Comic
Rebethany: Early twenties

Rebethany is a sweet and syrupy Southern belle, who has just been arrested for murder. She is talking to a TV reporter. Eventually, she does get around to telling the reporter why she did it, after telling them this story.

REBETHANY: Hi. My name's Rebethany. Rebethany Anne Chastain. I know, it sounds British, don't it? Yeah, my momma was from England. No, not the country. You know, New Hampshire? *(Pause)* God, that's a long ways away. My daddy was Alabaman, born and raised. Except then he moved to Arkansas when he was two, so I guess he wasn't really raised here actually. Although . . . Well . . . Does that count as being raised here if you were two? I don't know. Anyway, they were good people, maw and paw. Very good people. *(Pause)* Until the drought came. Summer a '97. I'll never forget it. Paw came in one day saying, "Who let the dang hose run dry?!?" Of course, I had done it. I was cleanin' off my bicycle, on account'a it was dusty. You see, we live in a dirt road, all a' way up in Elmer, nearest to Kentucky? And I was really proud of my bicycle. I was the only girl in Elmer with a bicycle! At least one with wheels on it. Of course Maybelline Ohmer had a bicycle also, but it was just a frame. She found it at the old church yard, underneath a pile of leaves. The bishop said she could have it if she'd finish cleanin' up the leaves. Of course she did it. Maybelline Ohmer had to have everything. We were all so jealous. It didn't even have a seat or nothing. It was just a frame. But lord, she'd sit on that thing for hours. No wonder she got tetanus in her leg that summer? And she lost control of her vagina. I swear, the entire cooch just fell right off of her! Least that's what her boyfriend Russell told me. And he should know, cuz he was her brother. Anyway, daddy came home one day, and he'd made a bundle, playing poker? And he came up to our double wide with a brand new shiny bicycle for me. With a seat and everything! So I used to ride that bike past Maybelline Ohmer's house every morning before school. And I'd say, 'Hey Maybelline! How's that frame of yours doing?' And she would call me dirty names. I mean, really un-Christian-like things, you know? Until one day Maybelline stopped coming out. I thought, 'Surely her momma must be spankin' her for all them nasty things she said.' But no, come to find out, it was just her vagina fallin' off.

(She folds her arms.)

I guess that was just God's way of punishing her for all them nasty things she said.

Dramatic
Viktorya: Late twenties, Polish

Viktorya works as a maid for a seemingly wealthy family who own a hunting lodge in upstate New York. She was from a wealthy family herself until World War I began. She is commenting on a member of the family's statement that Americans have no idea how lucky they are.

VIKTORYA: He is right. No one in America knows. It is like a miracle here. You wake up, it is quiet. In the air, you smell nothing burning. You have horses here that have not been eaten by starving people. When there is thunder and lightning, it is only thunder and lighting. In a way I am glad to know people can still feel as confident as you do. My own brothers sounded just like you. But that was 1914. When the Austrians come to Przemysl, my city, a Polish boy—a soldier who we hid in my house, this is long story I won't bore you with—the Austrians, they take, take, take, they are very polite, very clean, but all they do is take, all our food; you can imagine, we are hungry. This Polish boy—he is afraid if he sneak out to find the Polish army they shoot him as deserter, but if he give himself up to Austrians they hang him as spy. Anyway, he has hundreds and hundreds of cigarettes—we don't ask where he got them—he teached us all to smoke: me, my younger brother (my father and older brothers, already they were maybe killed I think, to answer your question) so to take away the hunger we sit with the Polish boy at night in our attic and watch the shelling at the front and smoke cigarettes.

Information on this playwright may be found at www.smithandkraus.com. Click on the AUTHORS tab.

Seriocomic
Penelope: Mid to late forties

Penelope is running for office in Nebraska and is giving a campaign speech. This is the end of it.

PENELOPE: I believe that you deserve happiness. I want you to feel good about yourself and what you are doing on this planet. I want you to have indulgent hobbies, brilliant children and/or pets, secret pleasures and a life filled to the brim with good memories to take with you when the time comes for God to snatch you from life and send you into nothingness. I say we get together and shove my opponent's plans for up his hoo ha cause I, Penelope Easter, will fight for your happiness. Will you fight for mine? I do not believe in Anger. Guilt. Powerlessness. Restriction. Oppression. I do not believe in being scared. That's who I am so let me ask again, who are you? You know what I'm going to do. Who are you? You know it in your hearts that this woman before you's gonna cook up one hearty stew for Nebraska. What're you bringing to this potluck? You gonna help me cook? You gonna set the table? You gonna pour me a glass of wine while I brown this meat? While you're at it you wanna make the bed? You wanna get in bed with me? You wanna see what kind of magic we can really make? Well C'MON NOW let's cozy up in this Nebraskan King-size we're all oiled up in and work together for a *tomorrow* so bright that it can tear down tyranny with its beams of light. A tomorrow so clear that it can out sparkle the inky coal menace of entropy and decay. A tomorrow so hot and rich that it can pour hope like molten gold from a cauldron coating every step of our future. Together, let us march down our golden roads with the hard fought confidence that nobody can break

us and nothing can stop us. We shall boldly stroll into
our dreams and we *we* will not fall, we will not fail, we
will not look down cower nor cry cause you got me and I
got you and together we will find Life Liberty Happiness
and Freedom. Freedom From Fear!

Seriocomic
Francine: Thirties

Francine is the campaign manager for a woman named Penelope Easter who is running for office in Nebraska. Francine has written a speech for Penelope which really wowed 'em. "FFF" is the slogan Francine has come up with: Freedom From Fear.

FRANCINE: Oh my god, that room. The way that they . . . Groups of women crying. Men clumped together with their fists in the air, refusing to put them down. Some kid spray-painted F F F on a trash barrel, poured ethanol in it and lit it on fire. I thought they were going to rip the platform to shreds. Tear down the podium. Start an orgy. I don't even remember writing it. We were talking, it seemed hopeless and impossible and then it just all of a sudden blew up inside of me. Then out of me. All at once. Words, images, flow, shooting out and I can't even tell you where they were coming from. Preconceptions out the door. Precedents. Formulas. Do's and don'ts forgotten. Thinking? Oh No. No goddamn stupid motherfucking thinking. I wasn't thinking at all when I wrote it! It's the best speech I have ever written. That. *That* is my new standard. I can never go back. And she fucking killed it. Oh my god. Slaughtered. Nailed. Fucking virtuoso Yitzhak Penelope Amazing fucking Easter fucking god damn shit water I need more water!

Seriocomic
Rita: Fifties

Rita and her friend Jimmy, a female impersonator (he pre-
fers to describe himself as a "tribute artist") have cooked
up a plan to get their hands on the townhouse of an ec-
centric old woman named Adriana who has died. Jimmy
is impersonating Adriana. Rita, a real estate broker, has
been to an open house for another, similar townhouse and
thinks she can make a big score. The Christina she refers
to is Adriana's niece, who comes into Adriana's house upon
her death. Rita and Jimmy are hoping to get Christina to
split the money from the sale of the townhouse. Of course,
Christina still thinks Jimmy is her aunt.

RITA: Well, hold onto your teeth, kids. After I left work this
afternoon I passed by that eyesore of a dilapidated townhouse on Barrow Street that's been for sale for the past
millennium. That evil twat Celeste is the broker. She's
like the negative version of me. As fate would have it,
today was the open house. I saunter in very nonchalantly
just as Celeste and her potential buyers are traipsing
through Hell House. I recognized this woman, Evelyn,
the wife of a fabulously wealthy hedge funder, lingering
by the dumbwaiter. I seize the moment! When no one is
looking, I edge over to her and say without any rancor,
"Can you believe what that Celeste is trying to get for
this shit hole?" Evelyn concurred that the place had no
pizazz, no je ne sais quoi and no moldings. Contrary to
what my enemies might say, I am a brilliant broker. I
paint a picture. I give my clients a glimpse of a glorious
future. Can we just say it? I am an artist! So I tell her
"You're looking for a one family townhouse? I got one.
Wedding cake ceilings, French doors, backyard garden."
When I told her about the skylight on the top floor, she

started frothing at the mouth. Frothing like a mad dog. She's willing to drop fifteen million for the right property. I might be able to start even higher. Christina, would you please say something?

Seriocomic
Sabra: Early thirties

Sabra is introducing herself to the other characters, who have all moved into the same apartment building. One of them, a teenaged girl called Kid, is writing a blog about them. Sabra is unnaturally upbeat and probably hiding something.

SABRA: I'm from back East I was living in Boston I went to school in Boston my family is near Boston I know Boston really really well don't you hate driving in Boston? There are some awful people in Boston I liked Boston but I wanted a change a big change a new start a fresh beginning something really non-Boston give me a new city a new lease a new opportunity for love and happiness and then I got this job I came here for a job and it's a great job organization It's so great to move duffel bags for something big I pick up duffel bags, don't look inside, and move them for a good cause. Which feels really good. And I get to see a lot of the city and I love this city oh my god I love this city The atmosphere the people the food Oh my god the foood and Wow we don't have hills like this in Boston I am working up a sweat here a good sweat I love sweat. Sweat means I am really excited to be here.
    (beat)
What do you do?

Dramatic
Ilsa: Thirties

The scene: A nearly empty bar. Ilsa sits alone at the bar. After a moment she turns towards the audience, speaks softly.

ILSA: I always know them; well, I can usually spot them, right away. It's like a sixth sense or something. They're usually the ones talking too loud, making with the jokes, laughing too loud. Talking; talking to . . . whoever's around, next to them, next bar stool. Maybe their friends, maybe not. Maybe they're people they just met, I don't know, doesn't matter. So I sit, and wait, and watch. I want to be sure. I like bars that are bars, not clubs or lounges. Just good old-fashioned *drink bars* where people can sit and talk and hear. And the lighting's usually dim, and the music's not too loud. So soon I'll have a drink or two to loosen up. As I continue to watch them. I need to be certain. By now I know all the signs. As the night goes on, they get louder and their laughter . . . It's usually around then that I mosey over, get closer, a bar stool nearby. Let them see me, know I'm there. By now they're up on their drinks and are very accepting of all new friends. And so I ingratiate myself, let them know I think they're funny; as I laugh at their unfunny jokes. As the drinks keep coming. And soon, well sooner rather than later, the two of us become engaged in some frivolous conversation about . . . doesn't matter. So I suggest that we move away from the bar, somewhere quieter. "Sure, they'll say. And we do. Perhaps to a darkened corner somewhere, or maybe a small out of the way table. And soon, somewhere in that shadow, I look into their eyes and ask, *(Very softly, caring)* "So . . . what's going on?"

Perhaps it's how I say it; like I mean it, like I really want to know. Because usually at that moment, their expression changes, they look at me as if . . . as if for the very first time. I mean here we've been talking . . . And so I say it again, "What's going on? Tell me." Then there is that moment where the tide changes, where the curtain opens. Where everything is different than it was just a moment before. And then they talk, begin *really* talking; but now their voice is much softer.

(beat)

Sometimes . . . sometimes it's about grief. Sometimes, it's about the end of a long love affair or a marriage that ended. Or sometimes it's about something that happened a long time ago—something that still haunts them. But it always seems to be about loss. Pain. And then they talk, and talk and talk. But they usually speak very softly. —And then they cry; almost always. And sometimes I cry with them. Maybe even hold their hand. Finally . . . I feel. Finally I feel what . . . !

(beat)

And sometimes they make these small childlike sounds. Not words, but sounds. And I sit there, and listen, and let them know I'm there. Because in that moment, I care— very much. We are not strangers anymore. And we both sit there until, well, there's nothing more to say, so we're silent for a while. There's just bar noise and music. And perhaps someone else laughing too loud at the bar. And I know it's time for me to go. And I do; without much fanfare. Sometimes I tell them my name, my first name. And sometimes I don't. I just leave, smile, say good night, wish them the best. And then I go . . . home.

Information on this playwright may be found at www.smithandkraus.com. Click on the AUTHORS tab.

Comic
Moxie: Twenties to Thirties

TROPICAL HEAT, *set on a South Seas island during the 1920's, is an over-the-top comedy about a grandiose missionary who falls for woman of easy virtue, Moxie. In this speech, responds to the preacher, who has just admitted he loves her. She explains why she won't give up her wanton ways.*

MOXIE: I was only eighteen when we met. I was as pure as the driven snow. And he was a man with a shovel. His parents insisted he marry someone else, a girl from the right side of the tracks. But he returned to the wrong side of the tracks and tracked me down. He never loved her, but he loved me . . . *eight* times a night. When his parents found out about me, they forbid him from seeing me. He didn't know what to do, and so he enlisted. I was so angry I told him I wished he would die. And then he did. If only I had told him to sprain his ankle! After he died, my life turned completely sour. I lost my job, my friends, my savings. Soon I was flat on my back. Then I learned I *liked* being flat on my back. That's why I lead the type of life I live, Collar Man. I want to spend eternity with the only man I ever loved. And the only way that'll happen . . . is if I go to hell.

Dramatic
Julie: Twenty-eight

Julie has met her father, Dan, previously unknown to her, for the first time. Alone with Dan's wife, Julie expresses her feelings and her confusion on how to handle the situation.

JULIE: Sometimes, he'll say something and I'll note the inflection in his voice, or a gesture, or a mannerism, and I think "That's me. This guy is mimicking me," and then I realize—I got that from him. It's kind of weird. I guess I had an inkling that there might be more to it . . . than what I knew. His name isn't on my birth certificate, so, well, it made me question my mom's story. She didn't talk about it. She just said it was in the past and we needed to move forward. I guess a big part of me just moved on. I thought about looking for more info on him, but I didn't have much to go on. I'm still trying to get past the whole, "Why did you hide my daddy?" thing. I don't know how I would have dealt with that . . . if I had been in her shoes. Of course, it's easy to say what should have happened, but if there's anything that the Army taught me, it's that you never can be sure how you'll respond until you come face to face with the problem. I knew a girl in high school who was adopted, and when she was sixteen, she went through this huge effort to find her birth parents. It seemed crazy to me for her to spend time and money trying to find people who chose not to be in her life. My roommate in college was really close to her family, even though they were constantly making her mad. Her mom did all kinds of passive aggressive stuff and her dad didn't pay her much attention, and she would constantly complain about how awful they were . . . . and yet, she would call them almost every day and spend every weekend with them and her sisters—who were even worse. I figure I would rather spend time with people I like—and just because I'm related to somebody doesn't mean I like them. *(pause)* I don't want to hurt Dan, but I have no idea how to—I don't know, I don't even know what we're supposed to do.

Information on this playwright may be found at www.smithandkraus.com. Click on the AUTHORS tab.

Dramatic

Candice: Forty-eight

After revealing to Dan that that she dropped out of college because she was pregnant with Dan's baby, Candace introduces Dan to their daughter, Julie, now 28. After a couple awkward meetings, Dan asks seeks advice on connecting with her. Asked about her childhood, Candace tells Dan about Julie as a little girl.

CANDICE: I'm not sure what to tell you. She's always had a mind of her own, kind of like she had a plan and no one was going to get in her way. She was a good student, graduated from college before she turned twenty-one. I'm not bragging—it's not like I had a lot to do with it. Once I saw her out in the backyard—she was probably five— she was wearing a tutu and carrying a large plastic pirate sword. And she was dancing about, singing a song—"It's a Sunny Day, It's a Fighting Day." I still remember the tune—I'd sing it for you, but I can't sing worth a damn. She's always been very imaginative—once told me a story about a far off country where the sky was green and the grass was blue and all over the country side there were these giant cows—pink cows—which didn't give milk. Instead they gave soda pop, all different flavors of soda pop. And nearby was a little town, with big walls surrounding it that were all made of fruitcake. And the people in the town had never had soda pop because they were afraid to go out of the town because of a giant who lived on the hillside. Apparently the giant watched the cows or something. Anyhow, in the town was a little girl who really wanted some Dr. Pepper, and so she dug through the wall of fruitcake, by eating her way out, and snuck up to the herd of giant pink cows and drank her fill of Dr. Pepper until she was burping, and she burped so loud that she woke up the giant and he came to check on the herd and found her.

Information on this playwright may be found at www.smithandkraus.com. Click on the AUTHORS tab.

Dramatic
Samar: Eighteen to Twenty-five

Samar is an Egyptian Muslim, eighteen to twenty-five years old, who does not wear a veil. She dresses in chic, western clothes. She is a student at the American Egyptian University, studying journalism, and wants to work for the NY Times. *She is well off, cosmopolitan, speaks Arabic, French and English and is very friendly, very outgoing, political but also a party girl. She is delivering this monologue to a video camera to post on her internet blog. Together, she and her American roommate Intisar are making blog videos addressing women's issues and, in particularly, the controversial custom of veiling. So, in essence, she is addressing the world.*

SAMAR: There is a saying here in the Middle East about educating women. That it is like allowing the nose of a camel into the tent, that eventually this beast will edge all the way in and take up all the room inside. This really gets my goat. The same saying, yanni, might also be applied to the higeb, to the niquab, edging their way into my country, along with these antiwomen ideas. Covering a woman completely so no one can see her. It is not so much the higeb that frightens me. It's the abaya, the niquab, the chador, the burka. Each covering a little more, each another inch of this camel's nose into our lives. My mother wore miniskirts on the streets of Cairo and no one cared. Now look at us. We don't dare to show our legs in the street. How does this happen? Inch by inch. No one is forcing this . . . yet. It is the weight of society, of public opinion, of the sheihks, of peer pressure, even of fashion! Wearing the niquab is easy. Anyone can slip it on and suddenly you are holy. Your sins are hidden. You are hidden. Without the niquab you must rely on yourself to be modest, you must draw the holiness from within your soul. I believe that many women wear the veil for their beliefs, however, I also believe that many now wear the higeb and the abaya as a protest, a political statement that we must break from the West. It was the same in Iran during their revolution, women put on the higeb as a symbol. However, now, long after they have won, still the women are legally forced to wear this higeb. No longer a symbol of their freedom. I am happy that many schools in Cairo have banned abayas and niquab and I am proud to say that our university joins this ban. If we let the nose of this camel inside our school, soon there will be no room for women there at all. *Mish kida*? [Isn't it so?]

Dramatic
Edith: Forties to fifties

Edith is a jovial woman with a nervous energy that fuels her smile and keeps her talking about things she probably shouldn't. She is waiting at some sort of public travel location (airport, train station, etc.) and speaking to a fellow traveler. Her clearly unfortunate history with trips has her feeling anxious.

EDITH: I didn't like Henry. He was my husband but I didn't like him. Even still, there was no reason, not that there ever could be a reason for that kind of, I just have no idea what happened. I had this broken coffee pot in my hand and he was lying in the bed, wet sheets. But before I could even think about it, the storm shattered the windows in our room, rain pouring in and I fell backward as the wind swept through, knocking over furniture, shaking the room. Henry's body rolled off the bed and just disappeared over the edge of the broken window. Just gone. I dragged myself to the edge and looked over. His body had fallen all the way down and hit the concrete next to the pool. I could barely see it in the floodlights next to the emergency exit. It looked like several rooms had shattered windows on the lower floors and suddenly I became aware that my hands were being cut by the edges where the windows broke. Everyone was evacuated to the basement. That's where a very understanding paramedic named Jonathan bandaged my hands. Over hot chocolate, he told me several people had died because of flying debris or from falling. So there were other people who had . . . difficulties. The funny thing, well none of this is really funny, but the odd thing, one of the odd things, is that even now I have trouble being sad about Henry. I hate what happened, but there's some kind of fog around him in my head. It's almost like he never existed. Oh, but everyone at the hotel was so nice about everything, so apologetic. Like they could control the weather. They told me I could come back and stay anytime in the future, if that wouldn't be too painful. But I don't think I'll ever go back there. I'm not much of a "vacationer" anyway. Did I already mention that?

Dramatic
Holly: Forties

Julius Lee, a New York State Assemblyman, is running for Congress. When he was in college, his girlfriend Holly dumped him and Julius flipped out, menacing her. Holly has come out of the woodwork and threatened to go public with Julius' crazy behavior unless her husband gets a cushy political job. Here, the two meet for the first time since college. Julius has asked Holly to listen to reason. Holly responds.

HOLLY: You told me that you got a gun and were going to kill yourself. Do you remember that? No response. You sent me a picture of it. You'd show up at my classes, just sitting in the hallway looking crazy and miserable and I had to . . . walk by you like nothing was the matter. Do you remember that? You called me, blind drunk, screaming and crying, telling me weird stories that made no sense. You left things on the trails where I rode McGill, a backpack full of . . . I don't even know what. You broke into my room when I wasn't there. Do you remember that? You scared me so much! Half of me was always worried that I was going to hear that you shot yourself; half of me was scared that you would hurt someone else; half of me was afraid that you'd . . . to me . . . and I couldn't stop, and God help me I wanted to, God help me I tried. And that did something to me. I was the one that was supposed to move to New York or D.C. I was the one who had dreams that were going to turn into something. So, I'm sorry, if someone is going to ask me if you're decent; if you're right, I'm not going to say, "Yes!" Not unless I get something in return, and that something is my life back and that includes my husband! That includes my husband! You can save your, "I grew up in the slums, my parents were slaves, my playmates grew up to be sex workers" stories for someone else. Your life was fucked up. I don't care. Doesn't mean that anybody had less of a life because theirs wasn't fucked up before they met you. *(Beat)* You look at all those guys on the news, you look at that guy at Virginia Tech and tell me that you weren't five minutes away from being that guy. Okay. This is pointless. There are four New York City HUD positions now that are acceptable to us at this point. I saw that one just opened up. Why don't you have Mr. Berkshire, or someone else who actually has something to say, talk to me next time, okay? This is pointless.

Seriocomic
Nikki: Twenty-five

Nikki, an ex-dancer, nervous about the night, and about to have yet another hook up, tries to gain courage to open her heart again as she waits for Peter who picked her up earlier that night.

NIKKI: BE A FUCKING ADULT! That's what I wanted to scream at them. Fucking kids in the bar. Under age. You know they were. Nineteen year old piss ant shit faced—Don't. Don't stick up for them because they looked—. Because they were hot. With their *(mimics clothes)* and *(mimics faces)* Whatever insecure glittery shit is exploding all over your apple bottomed jeaned ass THEN TAKE THEM THE FUCK OFF YOU TRENDY MOTHERFUCKER. Because yes—this twenty-five year old knows how to act in this fucking "cruel, cruel world". And if you don't act like who you are— who you really are. This world will. Eat you. Alive. I should go home. I shouldn't be here. I will. Go home. I'll—. Thought that the minute you came over, started talking. The minute you
    (Imitates a simple gesture/movement that Peter did that impressed her.)
I was like "oh really" but wanted to. You are taking forever. Really? Really? It takes that long to fucking piss. You can't talk when you do it? That's insane. I talk when I shit all the time. Sometimes I find myself talking in the stall to myself. Other people. Depends on how much I take. I hate ecstasy. Sucks that's all you had. So nineties, whatever that was. My mom still only watches like Wynona Ryder movies. My mom's boyfriend, Phil: "Nikki you look just like her" but I think that's just because I shop lift. Phil. He's retarded. A fucking joke. He's fucking blind as a

bat but still shoots off guns in their backyard. He said he used to jerk off to her. Wynona Ryder. Kept pictures of her like under his bed in a shoebox. Now he's like forty-seven! Last class I took—"Deconstructing the Twentieth Century"—University of Chicago—my parents made me take fucking classes while at Joffrey—because how could I really make it—dancing—right!? "No one dances forever. Your body gives out—like that!—so you better be ready to figure out something else after."

Comic
Philipa: Nineteen

Philipa is talking to her McDonald's coworker, a hapless middle-aged man named Gil. She tells him how and why she is going to get a managerial job instead of him. Then she tells him how she's going to celebrate.

PHILIPA: See, the thing is, I'm a go-getter! I go, and I get! You don't need to be a dude, you don't need to be a slut, you don't need to graduate high school, all you need to know is what you want and go get it! I don't do coke, I don't do smack, and, now man, everything's coming up Philipa. Ten years from now, I'm gonna be like the manager of all McDonalds, and you know where I'm goin' after that? *(Beat)* Walt Disney World Resort. You ever been to Walt Disney World Resort? Course ya haven't. I have literally met no one who went to Walt Disney World Resort. I bought this Disney autograph book when I was five? And when I go to Walt Disney World Resort, I'm gonna meet the dude who plays that little naked kid in the Jungle Book? Mowgli? And I'm gonna fuck the shit out of him. And after we've finished, I'll get him to sign my autograph book. And then, whenever any basic bitch tries to shame me or make me feel lesser than her or whatever, I'll show them the autograph book and be like: What've you done, bitch? And that's when I'll know I've made it.

Information on this playwright may be found at
www.smithandkraus.com. Click on the AUTHORS tab.

You are Dead. You are Here

Christine Evans

Dramatic
Zaynab: Teens, Iraqi

Zaynab is a blogger, living in Fallujah. This is direct address to the audience.

ZAYNAB: Hello Earth. Greetings from Fallujah. The mud is getting wetter every day but Al-Chalabi says the situation is "calm and improving." Huh. We've all been cooped up here and the baby demon cries all the time. The boys still go out, Dad tells them not to, but my cousin Nasir does what he likes now and Mahmoud follows him. And I have to stay here with my crying aunt and her crying baby and my mother who is taking Prozac by the fistful but won't give me any and nobody can go near the windows since the car bomb last week. I hate babies. I'll never have a baby, especially in a war. Anyway things reached boiling point when the baby screamed and screamed, I was looking after it while Aunt Morouj slept, I shook it just a little bit to see if I could scare it quiet, but Auntie saw me and lost her mind and started shouting and slapped me, and I cried and my mother cried and as my Dad said, the house was full of howling females until he yelled at us to shut up. So I decided to do Mahmoud's job that he has stopped doing and take out the garbage, just to breathe my own lungful of air. I was in a very bad mood and wishing the baby and Nasir and my aunt would vanish back to Baghdad, but they can't because their stupid house was bombed. Anyway I stomped over to the garbage. It stank and it was overflowing so I wanted to hurry, but then I noticed a big round thing in the bin. It looked like a watermelon but it was reddish-purple, not green. I poked it with a stick to see what it was and it rolled over and I saw. It was a boy's head. I felt completely calm, as if I was made of ice. I noticed the green-blue bruises on his cheek. How young he was, his top lip soft and downy above the broken teeth. The curl of brown hair on his forehead. He was like a flower, truly, a little crushed but beautiful. His green eyes were open and they looked straight into me. And then I realized. It was Khalid, Nasir's friend. The furnace of Fallujah rushed back into my lungs and I retched. I ran back inside and couldn't talk, I just locked myself in the bathroom until I could stop being sick. What kind of world is this? What did Khalid do? He looked right into my eyes. And now I know something I will never be able to explain. I am so, so, terrified of what Nasir will do when he finds out. Aunt Morouj says we mustn't tell him. But that's one of the things I saw in Khalid's eyes. Nasir will find out. And then we will reap the wind.

Information on this playwright may be found at www.smithandkraus.com. Click on the AUTHORS tab.

Seriocomic
Meredith: Teens

Meredith, seventeen, sitting on a sofa with her boyfriend Jim, watching television late at night, in the dark, in a small town in east Ohio in the autumn of 1954. She is trying to find a way to tell him that she's pregnant. He doesn't want to hear it.

MEREDITH: I was hungry for peaches. I've been getting all kinds of weird cravings lately. And sometimes I can smell bacon frying when nobody is cooking bacon. And also I've been hearing these radio broadcasts in my head. I mean, not real ones. It's like, there's this special frequency and I'm the only one tuned to it, and I can hear these voices and sounds and this music. It's just like murmuring in the background all the time, and sometimes somebody turns it up, and I can hear parts of it really clearly, and then it gets all garbled again. I don't think it's from Mars. I don't know where it's from. And I've been having a lot of nightmares, really disturbing ones, and I wake up in the middle of the night all sweaty and shaking so I go downstairs and open the refrigerator in the dark, because I like to see the light streaming out of the refrigerator into the darkness, like a picture of God in my old Bible story book. I mean, if God is everywhere, then he's in the refrigerator, right? I think everywhere means everywhere. If you believe that sort of thing. I don't know if I do or not. But I keep getting this feeling there's things going on all around me that I don't quite understand. It's like I'm a radio and my reception isn't good enough to draw in everything that's zapping through the air, so I just get these fragments of dialogue, sudden bursts of revelation, like listening to the radio late at night. Which I do sometimes when I can't sleep and go downstairs and have an onion and anchovy sandwich at three in the morning, and maybe I don't want to go back to sleep, because I've been dreaming that rats are eating the baby or something. And also I keep losing everything. I lost my keys. I lost my driver's license. I lost the cat. Except that came back. I lost my virginity in the back seat of your Chevy during *The Creature From The Black Lagoon* at the Drive-In. That's not coming back. Some things you can find again and some things, once you lose them, they're gone forever. And that's a long time. As we learn from popular songs on the radio. Also, I believe in ghosts. Not like Caspar the Friendly Ghost or people wearing sheets like in Three Stooges movies or anything like that. I mean I can feel these presences all around me. Like watching us. Don't you ever get the feeling there's all kinds of presences around you, watching you?

To obtain a copy of the entire text of any play,
contact the rights holder.

T.I.C. (TRENCHCOAT IN COMMON) © 2012 by Peter Sinn Nachtieb. Reprinted by permission of Mark Orsini, Bret Adams Ltd. For performance rights, contact Dramatists Play Service, 440 Park Ave. S., New York, NY 10016 (www.dramatists.com) (212-683-8960).

TOURISTS OF THE MINDFIELD © 2012 by Glenn Alterman. Reprinted by permission of Glenn Altermann. For performance rights, contact Glenn Altermann (glennman10@gmail.com).

TROPICAL HEAT © 2013 by Rich Orloff. Reprinted by permission of the author. For performance rights, contact Rich Orloff (richplays@gmail.com).

UNDISCOVERED PLACES © 2013 by D. Richard Tucker. Reprinted by permission of the author. For performance rights, contact D. Richard Tucker (dave@drichardtucker.com).

VEILS © 2008 by Tom Coash. Reprinted by permission of the author. For performance rights, contact Tom Coash (thomascoash@sbcglobal.net).

VERY STILL & HARD TO SEE © 2012 by Steve Yockey. Reprinted by permission of Mary Harden, Harden-Curtis Assoc.. For performance rights, contact Mary Harden (maryharden@hardencurtis.com).

WARRIOR CLASS © 2012 by Kenneth Lin. Reprinted by permission of Chris Till, Creative Artists Agency. For performance rights, contact Dramatists Play Service, 440 Park Ave. S., New York, NY 10016 (www.dramatists.com) (212-683-8960).

WILD © 2013 by Crystal Skillman. Reprinted by permission of Amy Wagner, Abrams Artists Agency. For performance rights, contact Amy Wagner (amy.wagner@abramsartny.com).